ETpedia™

Young learners

500 ideas for English teachers of young learners

Vanessa Reis Esteves

Series editor: John Hughes

www.myetpedia.com

ENGLISH TEACHING *professional*

ETpedia
Young Learners

© Vanessa Reis Esteves

The authors have asserted their rights in accordance with the Copyright, Designs and Patents Act (1988) to be identified as the authors of this work.

Published by:
Pavilion Publishing and Media Ltd
Rayford House
School Road
Hove BN3 5HX
UK
Tel: 01273 434 943
Fax: 01273 227 308

First published 2016

ISBN: 978-1-911028-21-5

PDF ebook ISBN: 978-1-911028-50-5

Epub ISBN: 978-1-911028-51-2

Kindle ISBN: 978-1-911028-52-9

Author: Vanessa Reis Esteves

Editor: Penny Hands

Production editor: Mike Benge, Pavilion Publishing and Media

Cover design: Emma Dawe, Pavilion Publishing and Media

Page layout and typesetting: Emma Dawe, Pavilion Publishing and Media

Printing: Ashford Press

Contents

Introduction

10 reasons for using this resource

1. Everything in one place

English language teachers of young learners can find supplementary resources, teaching ideas, activities and tips in a multitude of places. The shelves of the staffroom may be full of published resource books and they may have access to folders of materials created by colleagues. Internet search engines provide links to thousands of websites offering instant lesson plans and ideas. The sheer amount of available material can be overwhelming, and finding a tip can be time-consuming. The aim of this book is to bring a collection of resources together in one place for faster reference.

2. Clearly organised

This resource contains 50 units covering everything from things you should know about young learners to activities for teaching a particular topic, suggestions for using songs, chants, rhymes, stories, drama and arts and crafts activities. Each unit lists 10 points. Why 10? Well, having a choice of 10 activities for the topic of animals and pets, for example, should provide most teachers with a broad enough range of options to enable them to prepare a lesson on the topic. Similarly, walking into your first ever young learner class having read about 10 activities for your first lesson could make all the difference to the way the children see you. Finally, having 10 ways of managing behaviour in the young learner classroom up your sleeve should improve your chances of avoiding problems and keeping your students motivated.

3. New teachers

If you are just starting out in your career teaching young learners, this resource will provide you with a range of practical activities to support you on your way. In particular, the section on things to avoid in the young learner classroom will help you start on the right foot.

4. Experienced teachers

If you have been teaching for a while, this resource may remind you of techniques and activities that you haven't used for a while, and give you fresh ideas for increasing your repertoire.

5. Supplementing your coursebook

If you are using a coursebook or a set of materials prescribed by your institution, this resource will help provide support by offering ways to lead into, expand or adapt them to suit your learners' needs and prepare them for the Cambridge Young Learners 'Starters', 'Movers' or 'Flyers' exams, which are aimed to help children in primary or lower secondary education improve their English.

6. Studying for an ELT qualification

Perhaps you are planning to take the Teaching Knowledge Test (TKT), or studying for another qualification, such as CELTA, a Cert TESOL course or the IH certificate in Teaching Young Learners. This book covers many of the topics and areas you will look at in the input sessions of your course, as well as giving you ideas for your teaching practice. Candidates taking a higher-level qualification such as DELTA, or a Diploma in TESOL, will find the lists of 10 especially useful as an aide-mémoire when preparing for the written examinations as well as a source of activities for lessons.

7. Teacher trainers

If you are a teacher trainer, senior teacher or director of studies who delivers staff training on a range of topics, use the checklists of ideas that this resource offers as a way to prepare your sessions.

8. Materials writers

The resource includes examples of activities for teaching specific topics frequently found in young learner programmes, so anyone developing their own materials for the classroom and keen to ensure a variety of activities for a specific topic will find it a useful reference.

9. Additional materials

There are photocopiable worksheets in the Appendix. These worksheets relate to certain units in the book and provide teachers with instant classroom activities. Many of them are also available in full colour, and these can be found at https://www.myetpedia. com/appendix-materials/. A series of video clips by the author are also available, demonstrating how to make some the craft materials that are included in the book. These are available at https://www.myetpedia.com/etpedia-videos/, and you will be guided to these as appropriate.

10. More time

No matter where they teach or what classes they are currently teaching, teachers more often than not feel that they need more time to plan, more time to search for resources, more time to reflect and develop and more time to focus on classroom teaching and the students. This resource will help teachers rise to this challenge by offering a collection of accessible, easy-to-use tips, suggestions, activities and ideas all in one place, allowing teachers to save their energy for the place where they are needed most – the classroom.

'These are the secrets I wish I'd known when I first started teaching young learners.'

Vanessa Reis Esteves, author of ETpedia Young Learners

Introduction

10 ways to use this resource

This resource has been written for people who teach English as a second or foreign language to young learners. It can be read and used in different ways according to your level of experience, needs or interests.

1. Cover to cover

You could start at the beginning and read to the end. If you are finding out about teaching English to young learners for the first time, then the resource will work as an introductory text to the subject.

2. Read a section

The contents page will direct you to the different sections. In each section, you will find units containing 10 ideas, tips, activities or thoughts on a particular aspect of teaching young learners. Some of these sections might not be immediately relevant to your context, while others will help you with immediate interests, concerns or questions.

3. Teacher's block

Just as writers sometimes have days when they can't write (a condition commonly referred to as 'writer's block'), there are days when teachers of young learners search in vain for ideas for a lesson. This resource aims to help with any episodes of 'teacher's block'. Open the book at any page and see if the ideas there give you inspiration.

4. Plan a lesson

Perhaps you are preparing a detailed lesson plan for a training course, or you feel that you want to hone your planning skills. If so, start by looking at Unit 9: 10 tips for planning a young learner lesson.

5. Write in the book

Maybe you've tried one of the activities in the resource or found an idea you liked. Make notes about why it worked or how you adapted it, so you can refer to it again later.

6. Help colleagues

If you work with other teachers, you've probably experienced a situation where a colleague is desperately looking for something to improve their lesson. Perhaps you can help them out by suggesting they manage a class of excited young learners using some of the ideas in Units 12 or 16. Or, if they'd like to tell a story in a lesson, share some of the storytelling suggestions in Unit 28.

7. Last-minute lessons

Most teachers have experienced a day when a colleague is off sick and they've been asked to teach their class at short notice. If this has happened to you, have a look at the section entitled 'Activities for topics' (page 97), which contains an abundance of topic-related activities to help you teach a complete and motivating lesson.

8. More practice

Many students require extra practice on specific areas of English. For example, they might need to practise English sounds, or perhaps you've noticed that a class needs to be made more aware of intercultural activities. Use this resource to help you enhance your lessons and engage your students.

9. Develop yourself

If you're at the stage of your teaching career where you feel you are ready for more of a challenge, you'll find some other titles and resources in Further Reading (page 131).

10. Write your own 10

Teaching is always evolving, developing and changing, so why not create your own 10 tips or pointers and share them with your colleagues? There is space to add your own tips at the end of the book (page 249).

'Teaching young learners gives you the opportunity to see the world through children's eyes and gives you a whole new perspective about learning and life in general.'

Norma Marcial, Mexico

Vanessa Reis Esteves ...

- ▶ has been working in English language teaching since 1996
- ▶ is currently a teacher, teacher trainer and author
- ▶ is a well-known presenter at international teacher conferences and associations
- ▶ runs workshops and delivers teacher training on behalf of schools, universities, publishers and the Portuguese Ministry of Education
- ▶ has co-authored coursebooks for young learners and teenagers in Portugal
- ▶ has written articles for magazines such as *English Teaching Professional*
- ▶ is a part-time teacher at *Escola Superior de Educação* in Porto, Portugal
- ▶ delivers training online via webinars and virtual learning environments
- ▶ teaches overseas teachers at the Oxford Teacher's Academy in Oxford every summer
- ▶ is currently working on her PhD in 21st Century Skills and Learning.

Thanks and acknowledgements

The 500 tips, ideas, ways and resources in this publication are based on the secrets that I have learned in my 20 years as a teacher, teacher trainer and author of classroom materials. The whole collection is a combination of new and original ideas with classic ideas and activities that get passed down from one generation of English language teachers to another. My deepest thanks, therefore, go to all the students, teachers, trainers and colleagues who have crossed my path and directly or indirectly helped in the creation of *ETpedia Young Learners*. In particular, thanks to John Hughes and Robert McLarty, who believed in me from the start, Cristina Bento, who was my guardian angel, and everyone at Pavilion Publishing and Media, especially my editor, Penny Hands, whose advice and suggestions were a godsend. Thank you to you all for making this dream come true.

Introduction

Preparation and planning

This section begins by sharing some useful things that you should know about young learners. Less experienced teachers will benefit in particular from finding out more about the role of an English teacher of young learners. They may also be keen to know about some things to avoid when teaching young learners, such as not taking the children's behaviour personally and continually changing activities and classroom routines.

The subsequent units focus on how to establish a safe and meaningful learning environment, and how to connect with the children you are teaching so that learning English becomes a motivating and engaging experience for everyone in the classroom.

The final unit offers some useful tips on how to plan a meaningful lesson for learners of this age group so that everyone leaves the classroom with a smile on their face.

Young learners are generally considered to be children attending primary school, which means that they are between six and twelve years old. Very young learners, on the other hand, are considered to be children attending nursery school, which means that they fall into a 3–5-year-old age group. When planning your lessons, remember that there are significant differences between younger young learners (6–8-year-olds) and older young learners (9–12-year-olds). Here is a list of 10 important differences for you to consider. Points 1 to 5 are about 6–8-year-olds and points 6 to 10 are about 9–12-year-olds.

1. Egocentric

The younger a young learner is, the more egocentric they are likely to be. Thus, when teaching younger young learners, remember to reserve a few minutes in each lesson for an activity which will allow the children to share things about themselves with you and to feel that your sole focus is on them. Also, remember to raise the children's awareness of the importance of group dynamics and how to work with others and respect each other's feelings.

2. Pre-logical thinking

Young learners in general, but particularly younger young learners, have serious difficulty in thinking logically and abstractly. This means that younger young learners will not be able to do two abstract tasks simultaneously, such as sorting out a list of words according to two categories. Thus, remember to plan concrete learning experiences with immediate goals in your lessons. Begin by asking them to sort the words in terms of the first category. Once they have finished that task, ask them to sort the words according to the second category. Make new vocabulary more meaningful by teaching it using binary opposites.

3. Emotion-driven

Younger young learners are very emotion-driven, as they have limited abstract logical reasoning skills. This means that you will have to appeal to their emotions rather than their thinking skills. Include activities like songs, games and stories, which will open the children's 'learning gates' to learning. Avoid doing any type of language awareness work, such as formally teaching grammar, as this age group is still not able to take on anything abstract.

4. Repetition

Younger young learners love repetition. This not only makes them feel safe, but also helps them remember and learn. However, they can get bored easily. Try introducing a novelty factor for every repetition exercise. This means tweaking the activity so that it's slightly different from the way they did it previously. For example, in a drilling exercise, you might get them to repeat the words first in a princess voice and then in a silly parrot voice.

5. Limited writing skills

Don't forget that younger young learners are not yet able to read and write in their first language, never mind in English. Thus, rather than presenting them with too many writing tasks, invest in oral learning and TPR (Total Physical Response) activities involving plenty of movement, which get the children to practise their pronunciation and have fun.

6. Curious

Older young learners aged between nine and twelve years are starting to become aware of the world around them and are curious to find out more about it. This means that they will enjoy learning English by following a CLIL approach (Content and Language Integrated Learning) and doing some science and geography in English.

7. Choice

Older young learners respond well to choice as this empowers them and makes them feel more in control. One strategy that you can use is to present them with three activities and invite them to choose which two they want to do in that lesson.

8. More social

As young learners get older they start to become more social. This means that 9–12-year-olds are ready to start doing simple pairwork and groupwork activities when learning English. Try giving them a groupwork task or project to work on that they will then present to the class. Remember to guide them through the various steps and to explain clearly what you expect of them. This will keep the children focused and on track.

9. Literacy skills

As young learners become older they learn to read and write. This means that you can appeal to the fact that they love stories and bring along a few readers for fast finishers to read in class.

10. Roleplays and structured dialogues

Older learners still need structured tasks like roleplays or structured dialogues which they can adapt according to their likes and their experience of the world. This type of task also appeals to their imaginations and helps them apply and demonstrate their knowledge of the language and collaborate with others, which they enjoy doing at this age.

'Older learners are worried about being correct and using the right form of the language, while young learners are more spontaneous and enjoy trying English in order to practise a new way of communicating.'

Gabriela Dias Yamasaki, Brazil

Unit 1

10 things you should know about young learners

Young learners belong to an age group which is generally very motivated and eager to learn. They come to school with a big smile on their face and high expectations for your time together, and they love treating you with their special drawings and gifts. Here are 10 tips to get you thinking about how best to approach teaching young learners and how to cater for their basic learning needs.

1. Work with their energy

Children are very energetic. Their energy often lasts the whole day. Don't fight this. Use it in your favour to get them actively playing and learning in your classroom. Make sure that you plan various energetic activities for every lesson, for example, playing a game, singing a song or doing a drama activity.

2. Respect their attention span

When planning your lesson, bear in mind that a child's focused attention span is believed to be between 5 and 10 minutes. Thus, make sure that you introduce a new activity approximately every 10 minutes. So if you are teaching a 60-minute lesson, for example, plan six different activities for that lesson.

3. Use stirrers and settlers

When choosing activities for your lesson, remember to mix and match stirrers and settlers. Stirrers get children working and playing with each other actively; settlers give children individual quiet time and the opportunity to assimilate the language they have just been exposed to. Follow a stirrer with a settler to get the children to calm down, and to help you avoid behaviour problems and classroom management issues. For more tips on classroom management and ideas for stirrers and settlers, see the section entitled 'In the classroom'.

4. Use their imaginations

Children are eager to learn, and they are very imaginative by nature. Remember to capitalise on their strong imaginations and natural creativity to help them learn language. When doing a language activity, ask a question or two that will help children tap into their imaginations. These questions will help children acquire language in context while developing their imaginations and creativity in a stress-free environment.

5. Let them play

Children love to play. Playing helps them develop social skills and learn more about the world around them. Make sure that in each lesson you have at least one playful activity which helps them acquire language in context in a natural and fun way.

6. Work on social skills and emotional intelligence

Children are generally quite self-centred. This means that you need to help them develop essential social skills. Remember to present children with learning opportunities and activities which require them to practise and use your target social skills.

7. Negotiate clear rules

Children need clear rules and boundaries in order to feel safe in the classroom. Chat with them about the target behaviour that you both need to keep in mind in order to be able to play and learn together. Then choose five rules which target that behaviour. When a rule has become automatic, you can substitute it with another rule that you want the children to work on. For more ideas, see the section entitled 'In the classroom'.

8. Praise children

Always focus on the successes and appropriate behaviour that happen in class, rather than on the less positive things. When you see good behaviour, reward it by saying something like, 'Class, did you notice how Carlos put his hand up and waited for his turn? Wow, Carlos! What a star! Now what did you want to say?' Carlos will feel proud of himself and the class will realise that if they want to get your attention, this is the type of behaviour they have to replicate.

9. Introduce routines

Routines are important because they give children the opportunity to excel, and they give the teacher the chance to see the children behaving well in class. Remember that a routine may be the only activity that a child gets right in a particular lesson. Choose your routines wisely: start and end lessons with a routine like a lively hello song or chant to demonstrate to them that learning English is both achievable and fun.

10. Challenge children

Remember to make learning challenging and exciting. Make sure that the activities themselves are not as basic as the simple language they are learning. To stave off boredom, introduce activities that challenge them at a cognitive level, even if they require simple language. The language will be easy, but the level of thinking will keep them motivated, focused and on track.

'Before you start teaching a young learners class, make sure you establish clear rules and procedures and above all stick to them!'

Glenn Standish, Director of Studies, International House Toruń

Unit 2

As any teacher of young learners will tell you, you have to wear multiple hats to make sure that effective learning takes place in the classroom. Here are 10 roles that help you make a difference in the classroom and in your children's lives.

1. A surrogate parent

The teachers that we tend to remember as adults are not just the teachers who taught us lots of interesting facts and met all the job requirements, but those who also saw their pupils as people, and truly cared for them. Getting to know your students as well as you can and caring for them both in and out of lessons is an absolute must in the primary classroom.

2. A 'teachertainer'

It is no longer enough for teachers of young learners to be mere knowledge transmitters who teach the curriculum put together by an external entity. Teachers are expected to make learning engaging and fun. This means that many teachers see themselves as a mixture of teacher and entertainer – a 'teachertainer' – who makes a difference to the learning process.

3. A values transmitter

Children often spend more time at school than they do at home with their parents. Because of this, schools have taken on the role of teaching children basic values such as kindness, respect, sharing, being fair and polite, caring for the environment and respecting the world around them. Remember that in many cases, children will only hear about the importance of these values from you. So make sure that they find a way into your classroom and teaching.

4. A conductor

Primary school teachers are conductors in the classroom in the sense that they control learning for each child and prompt them to make new fun and exciting discoveries. Try to encourage children to make the right learning decisions, and only step in and help when it's absolutely necessary.

5. An organiser

Most children are very eager learners, but they are not autonomous enough to organise their own learning paths yet. Organise everything that happens in the classroom for them so that learning will become a logical and manageable process for everyone.

6. A facilitator

A primary teacher should plan lessons in a way that places the children at the centre of the learning process. This implies giving children strategies to become autonomous learners. See yourself as a walking resource, always ready to offer children the necessary language and tools to learn effectively.

Unit 3

7. A mirror and a mentor

Children watch our every move. They learn by the examples around them. This is why it is so important that, as primary teachers, we demonstrate the attitudes and reactions that we want our children to have in class. It is part of our role to accompany each child in his or her learning journey, and to act as a mentor who is able to challenge them at their level, thereby keeping their motivation to learn alive. Remember that children are curious by nature, so make sure you plan your lessons in such a way as to appeal to their natural curiosity.

8. An assessor

Great teachers are great assessors who are able to evaluate what children know and are already doing right. Rather than focusing on what children are doing wrong, try to focus on what they are doing right and what the next learning step is, ensuring that your feedback will make them want to come back into your classroom the next day.

9. A social worker

As teachers, we need to be aware that some of our children have complicated lives. Remember to be on the lookout for warning signs and, if necessary, to get help from professionals.

10. A form filler

There is a huge amount of paperwork that teachers need to fill in. As you fill in your learners' report cards, remember that the parent who is going to read it is eager to know how their child is learning, to find out what they need to do next and to hear at least one heartwarming thing about their son or daughter.

'Act as a facilitator and provide learning opportunities to allow the children to showcase their abilities and learn from one another.'

Solomon Au Yeung, Hong Kong

10 things to avoid in the young learner classroom

Good teachers teach children content, but great teachers know that they also have to teach with a heart. They know just how it is important to make children feel happy in the classroom and to 'open their learning gates'. Here are 10 tips to help you avoid some basic problems in the young learner classroom.

1. Avoid being too strict

Children need to feel safe and happy before they can learn. Being overly strict can 'shut their learning gates' for weeks. On the other hand, being their best friend can lead to loss of control. Try to establish clear rules for your classroom and to enforce them with a kind but firm hand.

2. Avoid speaking down to children

In order for learning to take place in your classroom, you will need to manage behaviour. Instead of reprimanding children or demanding good behaviour, try explaining the reason why that particular kind of behaviour is important. Building a climate of mutual trust and respect is the first key to learning in any classroom.

3. Avoid trying to control everything

Teachers need to manage and control what happens in the classroom without becoming control freaks. Remember that a lot of memorable learning happens when teachers take a step back and let the children experiment and come up with creative solutions. Have the courage to let go and allow the children to sit in the driver's seat.

4. Avoid taking things personally

As teachers, we tend to expect perfection in every lesson. When things go wrong, we quickly blame ourselves. While we do need to reflect on every lesson in order to maximise learning, we also need to remember that when children behave in a challenging manner, this doesn't necessarily mean that they don't like us or that we've done something wrong.

5. Avoid correcting every mistake

We want our children to learn English successfully and efficiently. The problem is that they keep making mistakes. Correcting every mistake causes children to become hesitant and less inclined to join in. They then quickly realise that if they don't say anything, the teacher won't 'pick on' them in front of the class. So, treat mistakes as if they were salt and pepper. Too little correction makes learning bland, but too much spoils the enjoyment. Only correct a mistake if it interferes with communication. If it doesn't, jot it down and deal with it later.

6. Avoid explaining grammar

Children are not yet capable of thinking abstractly. This means that they have trouble understanding grammar explanations. Rather than explaining grammar rules to children, teach them games or songs, which stay in their memory long after the lesson is over. Games and songs help them to pick up and practise the target language in a natural context while having fun.

7. Avoid the negative; mirror the positive

As teachers, we often act as children's role models. Children mirror the things we do and say. Thus, make a point of demonstrating positive examples like keeping the classroom tidy (with the children's help). Remember to focus on why this is important and how it helps them learn better.

8. Avoid having teacher's pets

It is natural to have more of an affinity with some children than with others. The secret is to make sure that this remains *your* secret. Make sure that you treat everyone the same. Remember how sad and frustrating it is to not be chosen because you aren't one of the teacher's favourites.

9. Avoid changing things every day

Resist the temptation to be overly creative, changing things every day. Remember that children like and need routine. Constant change makes it difficult for them to be well behaved because they are not sure what is expected of them. Remember that success feeds motivation!

10. Avoid doing or saying things only once

Children take time to learn and not every child is able to get things right after just one quick instruction. This means that before you ask children to do something for you, you need to demonstrate exactly what it is that you want them to do, rather than just telling them. Always invite two or three children to have a go at the task or activity in front of the class before you hand it over to the children.

> *'You must be a source of knowledge for your students, but do not try to be infallible. When you don't know something, find out for them and this teaches your students to search for knowledge.'*
>
> **Maciej Kudła, BASE language school, Poland**

Unit 4

10 ways to establish an exciting and purposeful learning environment

School can be something a child looks forward to or something they dread. To help ensure that the former is the case, here are 10 tips to help you make kids like school.

1. Get to know the children

Children enjoy going to school when teachers meet both their academic and their emotional needs. This means that you need to find out more about your students. Begin by making an effort to speak to them both in and outside the classroom. By connecting with them, you will soon understand them and their needs, and this process is likely to reduce behaviour problems. See Unit 6 for more on this.

2. Let them get to know you as well as each other

Invest time in allowing the children to get to know you as a person, and as a teacher. Share any personal details that you are comfortable with them knowing about. This will help create a special bond of trust between you. Invite the children to do pairwork and groupwork activities. These encourage them to get to know each other and develop social skills, which will have an impact on their working lives.

3. Decorate the classroom

Make the classroom look attractive and friendly. Display the children's work for everyone to see how good they are at learning English. To give the children more exposure to language, put up word cards that label the various objects and images in the classroom. Once they know a particular set of words, substitute them with new word cards to continue challenging the children.

4. Involve the parents

Remember that the children's parents are just as concerned about their children as you are. Involve them in the learning process by inviting them to come into the classroom to speak about their own hobbies, interests and jobs. Hold a meeting at the beginning of the year to explain what the children will be doing in the English classroom and why. When parents understand the goings-on of the classroom, they become assets in the children's learning process.

5. Create a time-out area

We all have our individual work rhythms and personalities, which can mean that some children finish a task before the rest of the class. Certain children may even reject an activity on a 'bad-behaviour day'. Rather than initiate a confrontation, try providing these children with an alternative learning experience or activity like reading a story quietly in the reading corner or completing a worksheet.

6. Create a friendly classroom environment

To create a friendly classroom environment, listen carefully to the children's opinions of the tasks and activities being done. You'll often find that they are able to come up with creative suggestions, which will help you engage them in class. Encourage them to respect each other's opinions by including and regularly referring back to a rule in the Rules and Consequences poster like: 'In our class we always listen to each other with our ears and hearts.' See Unit 11, point 4 for more on this.

7. Make learning relevant

Remember that we learn better when what we are learning is relevant to our experiences, interests, personalities and realities. When the content is abstract and theoretical, children tend to rote-learn it and then forget it. Focus on language they need in order to speak about the things in their lives; for example, family, food, pets, likes and dislikes, school, toys and games.

8. Set targets and celebrate achieving them

Make successful learning objectives concrete for children by setting achievable objectives and targets. Negotiate three to five learning targets for the week with the children. Reward the class's hard work and effort by celebrating when they achieve each target. This could mean playing the class's favourite game or singing their favourite song at the end of that particular lesson, or even giving them a sweet as a special reward for their hard work.

9. Support children with special needs

Remember to adapt general targets and objectives for children with special learning needs. Involve them in the process of defining their personal targets rather than simply presenting them with pre-defined targets. In many cases, they will know what they are capable of achieving better than you do, and if you have created a meaningful relationship with them, they will be motivated to tap into their 'super learning powers' to please you. The results are often surprising and can set a great example for the class.

10. Create attendance and punctuality awareness

Invest in promoting attendance and punctuality awareness. You can do this by being punctual for every lesson yourself, and by creating an attendance and punctuality chart, which a student fills in at the beginning of the lesson. Punctuality can then be objectively measured and rewarded.

Unit 5

10 ways to get to know your students

Before you can teach your students really effectively, you need to get to know them. Here are 10 ways to help you do that.

1. Speak to last year's teacher

The easiest way to find out about your students is to speak to last year's teacher. It is also a good idea to speak to other teachers at your school and your head of department as they may have valuable information to share with you. You should, however, bear in mind that the information they give you may be subjective, and that the student may behave in a completely different manner towards you. Always give students the benefit of the doubt.

2. Speak to parents

Parents are a good source of information. They know their children well and, like you, they are genuinely interested in their children's success and concerned for their well-being. To make sure that the meeting runs smoothly and is kept on an objective level, prepare it beforehand. Make sure that you take concrete examples and any facts and figures you may have so that you can prove your points objectively.

3. Speak to children both in and out of class

Remember that your learners are people with real lives and interests. Never miss an opportunity to go up to them and start a friendly one-to-one chat. Children soon realise that you genuinely care about them, which makes them bond with you. This will be reflected in their improved behaviour in the classroom.

4. Speak to the children's friends

Children often share their deepest feelings, worries and fears with their friends. If a child is very withdrawn and reserved, try finding out who their friends are, and asking them to help you learn more about the child you are concerned about. Remember to explain the reason why you are speaking to them and to keep the tone of the conversation light so that they will not feel threatened. You can end the conversation by letting them know where they can find you in case they think of anything that may be of interest to you later on.

5. Get-to-know-you activities

Young learners are not mature enough to work for themselves yet. In most cases they work hard to please their teacher. They are less likely to do this for you if they don't know you yet. Devote the first few weeks of the year to doing exciting and fun getting-to-know-you activities, which will set the tone for the rest of the year.

6. Invest in group bonding activities

Sometimes teachers ask children to work in pairs and groups, only to find that a certain child doesn't want to work with a specific student or group of students. Many children need to understand that they can learn by working with others. To avoid a situation in which children reject each other, get them to do group bonding activities, which help them discover that they share many interests with the other children in their class. This is the first step towards getting them to accept each other.

Unit 6

7. Make name cards

Learn the children's names as soon as possible. This will help you to keep a check on their behaviour and will prove to them that you care about them. To help you learn the children's names, get them to make personalised name cards: on one side, children write their name in big bold letters; on the other side, they write down three things they are happy for you to know about them. If children are not old enough to write, ask them to draw. The side of the card with their name will face the front of the class and the side with their personal facts will face them. As you come to their desk to help them with any doubts they have, you'll find out all sorts of interesting facts which will help you start a meaningful conversation with them.

8. Schedule show-and-tell sessions

As children start to become more comfortable with you and the class, set a day of the week for show-and-tell moments (see Unit 19). Children can bring things which interest them to class and share them with you. This will give everyone the perfect opportunity to ask interesting and meaningful questions and bond with each other.

9. Observe them in class

We all have different preferences when it comes to how we learn. Make sure that you plan a few pairwork or groupwork activities every week so that you are left free to wander round the class and observe the children: watch how they work, what type of activities they like doing, what difficulties they have, how they behave, etc. Jot down your findings to remind you how you can help each child and cater for their needs.

10. Be open!

A good way to get children to share personal information with you is to set an example. When children have worked hard, reward them by satisfying their natural curiosity and sharing personal details and stories about you and your family. You'll find that they'll drop whatever they are doing and listen attentively. They'll also start to see you as a real person and not just as their English teacher.

10 questions to ask about a new class

Each class you teach is unique, so begin the year by finding out as much as you can about them. Try using the following 10 questions to guide you.

1. What age are my students?

Establish whether you are teaching 'young learners' or 'very young learners' (see Unit 1). Young learners are often considered to be between the ages of six and twelve years old; very young learners are between three and five years old, and are usually still at pre-school. This distinction is important because young learners and very young learners have different skills and attention spans, and this will inevitably influence the activities you do and the planning of the lessons.

2. What is their first language and cultural background?

Asking the following questions will help you avoid culturally sensitive issues in class: 'What is my students' first language?', 'What cultural background do they come from?' and 'What cultural background am I teaching in?' For example, singing songs and listening to music is not common practice in all cultures, so you may need to substitute the songs in your coursebook with chants. These are often more culturally acceptable and still facilitate learning vocabulary and chunks of language.

3. How many children are there in the class?

The number of children in the classroom is another important factor to take into consideration when planning your lessons. If you are teaching a small class (7 to 15 students), you will need to plan more activities for each lesson than if you have a larger group of 20 or more students, who take a lot longer to get through activities. In larger classes, classroom management is an important factor to take into consideration when you are planning and giving your lessons, as you can easily lose control of the class with groups of this size.

4. What is their level of English?

Before going into the classroom, speak to your colleagues and head of department to find out things like whether this class is beginning to learn English or how much English they already know. Most classes are mixed-ability classes. Find out how many levels there are so that you can make important decisions regarding the most appropriate activities and interaction patterns to use. If this is not possible due to factors like staff turnover, give the children a placement test in the second week of lessons. Reserve the first week for getting to know the children and building a rapport with them.

5. How many times a week will I see them and where will I teach them?

Find out exactly how much contact time you have with the children each week, and what the school policy regarding homework is. Is homework common school practice? If so, how much homework is considered appropriate for the level you are teaching? You should also visit the classroom(s) you will be teaching in to get a better sense of the space and resources available. This will help you make important decisions regarding the type of activities and games you can do and technological equipment you can use.

6. Are there any children with special needs or allergies?

In order to help all the children learn effectively, find out as much information about each child as you can from the start. Are there any children with special needs in your class? What needs do they have? How can you cater for them? Begin the year with a parents' meeting and ask about special dietary requirements or any other special needs the children may have.

7. What skills do they already have?

Another important task for the teacher is to find out which skills the children have already mastered. Introduce pair or group activities, which allow the children to work together, leaving you free to wander around the class, observing them and recording your findings in your teaching diary. Look out for literacy skills. Can they already read and write in their first language and in English? If they don't use the Roman alphabet in their L1, introduce basic handwriting activities and invest more heavily in literacy tasks in class.

8. What activities do (or don't) they like doing?

Children don't learn a language for a specific purpose like ordering a meal in a restaurant or negotiating with clients in English. This means that you need to motivate them to learn the language by giving them activities to do which appeal to their natural learning curiosity, interests, learning styles and characteristics. Remember that young learners love to play. So introduce activities that involve play as often as you can.

9. What rules do I need to work on with this class?

As we discussed in Unit 2, point 7, children need rules and boundaries in order to feel safe and to learn efficiently. A happy classroom is a classroom where everyone can learn and play together in an orderly manner. This means that you need to find out which classroom behaviour rules already form part of your class's routine and which rules need to be introduced and worked on.

10. Will all the children in the class have a coursebook and a workbook?

Begin by checking if the school has adopted a coursebook and a workbook for the levels you are teaching. If not, you will be expected to come up with the material required for each lesson.

'The questions always in the back of my mind are: what are their expectations of me and my lessons? Are they going to like me and my teaching activities? Are they going to have fun with me? You can worry about lots of different things about your class but I truly believe that if you focus your attention on your students and what they expect to learn from you (and not just a syllabus), you'll be able to create a positive learning environment.'

Cristina Bento, Portugal

10 ways to determine students' likes

To be able to cater for your students' needs, it's important for you to discover how they like to learn English as soon as possible. You can do this by speaking to children informally or by conducting quick class interviews. Another option is to give them a questionnaire (see Appendix p138), which they can fill in by colouring smiley faces according to their feelings and preferences. Here are some topic areas that you could use as a starting point.

1. Direct questions

If the children have studied English before, you can start by asking them direct questions such as 'Do you like learning English?' and 'Which words or sentences can you remember?'

2. Favourite skills

Learning English implies working on the four skills, which are covered by coursebooks. Include questions relating to which skills they like to practise while learning English by asking questions like 'Do you like reading stories in English?' or 'Do you like listening to songs in English?'

3. Favourite activity types

Children will have favourite activities depending on how they prefer to learn. So ask them questions or give them 'like' statements about which activities they like doing in the classroom, for example, 'Do you like playing games?' or 'I like playing games.'

4. Phonics and literacy skills

Some children like to learn English by finding out more about the sounds and letters of the language. A phonics approach will allow them to do so by helping them associate English sounds with letters, thereby developing their literacy skills. If your coursebook does not include a phonics section, there are plenty of resources online which will help you find out more about introducing a phonics approach to learning in the classroom.

5. Autonomous work

Some children like to learn by having quiet thinking time in which they can work on their own to assimilate new knowledge and information. Remember to find out which children learn better in this way by asking questions like 'Do you like to work on your own?' or by giving them a 'like' statement such as 'I like working and doing tasks on my own'.

Unit 8

6. Pairwork and groupwork

Children who like working with others will be keen on pairwork and groupwork activities. Include a question or two to find out whether your students still work best in pairs or whether they are ready to take the next step and start working in small groups.

7. Sharing personal information

'Show and tell' is a traditional primary-level activity that allows children to speak about themselves and share personal information in a simple and non-threatening way. You can include a question relating to this popular activity in your questionnaire to find out whether your students are comfortable with sharing something about themselves and speaking in English in front of their peers.

8. Using resources

There is a huge variety of resources available to children learning English: coursebooks, workbooks, picture dictionaries, student grammars, apps, online practice exercises and Learner Management Systems (known as LMSs). Include a question or two to find out which resources your students like are used to, and feel comfortable using.

9. Finding out about the real world

Over the past decade, many schools have begun to invest in 'CLIL' (Content and Language Integrated Learning). This approach allows children to learn English while they find out more about the world around them through subjects like maths, geography, the arts and science. Find out what your students' favourite subjects are and whether they are used to learning in this manner.

10. Doing research

The internet has given children access to a wealth of information, allowing them to research and share information about topics of interest to them with others all over the world. Include a question or two about independent research work and student participation in online communities such as blogs and protected social media sites.

'If you produce a lesson that is exciting enough to get the kids fully engaged, you have an amazing time. They embrace any language games, and watching the shy children taking part feels great.'

William Reynolds, teaching in China

ETpedia: Young Learners © Pavilion Publishing and Media Ltd and its licensors 2016.

Unit 8

10 tips for planning a young learner lesson

Unit 9

When planning your lesson, remember to think about the characteristics of young learners and how you can cater for them. A good lesson presents young learners with activities that respect their short attention span and lets them play and have fun while learning. Here are 10 tips to have you planning engaging lessons that are fun for everyone.

1. Include an opening routine

Routines make children feel safe by letting them know what is expected of them and how they can please you. Start your lesson with a routine to guarantee that every child begins your lesson on a positive footing. One possibility is to use a lively 'Hello song' that gets the children in a good English-learning frame of mind and sets the tone for your lesson. There are many great songs on YouTube that you can choose from. An alternative is to use a chant (see Unit 22).

2. Plan a revision activity

Children need lots of revision to remember the language that they learn. To help them revise and practise language while having fun, start your lesson playing a game or singing a song that revises the language that they learned in the previous lesson. For game suggestions, see Units 34–36.

3. Choose learning objectives for your lesson

Before you begin planning the tasks and activities for your lesson, take a step back and look at the bigger picture. Which general learning objectives do you want to work on in that particular lesson? Do you want to develop children's self-study skills, their thinking skills, their intercultural knowledge or their imagination and creativity? This will help you choose the best language tasks and activities for your lesson. Remember to keep things within the children's capabilities.

4. Determine the language and skills content of your lesson

Once you have decided on your learning objectives, ask yourself the following questions: (1) which skills and language do I want to teach them today: reading, writing, listening or speaking? and (2) do I want to teach new words or a new language function? Once you have determined the language and skills content of your lesson, choose tasks and activities which help the children to achieve that aim.

5. Include activities that change the pace of the lesson

As you choose activities for your lesson, make sure that you include a few stirrers and settlers to manage the children's energy levels throughout the lesson. For further information about stirrers and settlers, see Unit 16. Remember to change activities approximately every 10 minutes in order to cater for children's limited attention spans.

6. Limit your creativity

Teachers are often creative by nature, but be careful not to be too creative, as children may feel threatened by too much change in a lesson. When you choose tasks and activities for your lesson, remember to repeat task types and activity types. When they are doing a familiar task or activity, children have the opportunity to focus on and acquire new language. In this way, learning English is safe and achievable for everyone.

7. Plan for success

Learning a language is difficult. To keep your children motivated, make them feel like they are succeeding and progressing in every lesson. Plan to include at least one confidence-boosting familiar activity in every lesson, one at which you know the children will succeed. This will give you the opportunity to praise and reward their success!

8. Follow a PPP (Presentation, Practice, Production) model

One way to structure your lesson is to follow a PPP model of learning. Start off by presenting new language to the children. Then choose a controlled activity such as a drill, which helps the children practise the language in a safe context. As the language becomes automatic, allow them to start experimenting and playing with that language. A 45-minute lesson plan may be structured as follows: lesson routine and revision activity: 10 minutes, presentation of new language in context: 10 minutes, controlled practice activities: 15 minutes, a freer practice activity: 5 minutes, closing routine and self-evaluation: 5 minutes. See the Appendix for a sample lesson plan (p139.).

9. Plan for variety

Your students won't always respond in the same way to different activities, so try to vary the lesson to suit everyone. For example, include a song or a chant, a flashcard activity and games with lots of movement so students aren't always in their seats.

10. Plan student-centred lessons

Centre your lesson around your students. Let them speak and play with English in class. Remember that they should be the stars of the lesson and not you. Teachers should be guiders and facilitators of learning rather than dictators who dominate the majority of the lesson.

'With young learners, routines and patterns are essential as they help children to feel more secure and to know what they are expected to do.'

Mariana Lampreia, Portugal

Unit 9

In the classroom

This section focuses on how to engage children from the very first day you teach them. Less experienced teachers in particular will benefit from the tips provided on how to manage and deal with the children's behaviour, establish routines and give instructions so as to maximise the learning that is going on in the classroom.

This section then moves on to look at how to manage the children's energy, suggesting activities for starting and ending lessons as well as giving you examples of various stirrers and settlers that young learners respond well to.

The final units offer some useful tips on appropriate classroom language to use when teaching young learners and practical suggestions on how to approach and deal with 'show and tell'.

10 activities for your first lesson

The way that you begin your first lesson is very important and will set the tone for the rest of the year. Because first impressions really do count, make sure that you create a positive impact on your students. Here are 10 activities that will help you do that.

1. 'Simon says' getting-to-know-you game

A simple way to start the year while allowing the children to have fun and get to know each other is by playing 'Simon says'. Organise the children in two rows on opposite ends of the room so that they can all see each other. Stand in the middle and give instructions like: 'Simon says hop on one foot if your favourite colour is green.' After a while, try to catch children out by leaving out the 'Simon says' part of the instruction. If a child follows the instruction, he or she is 'out'. An easy follow-up activity is to count and record the children's answers/reactions on the board and get them to make a class fact file about themselves to display in the classroom.

2. Ball game

For a fun way to learn each other's names, stand the children in a circle. Start off by getting a child to introduce him or herself (eg 'Hi, I'm Juan'), and to pass the ball to the child on the right. The second student repeats the first student's name, and adds his or her own name (eg 'He's Juan and I'm Isabella'). Start a new chain after about eight names, as it becomes too cognitively challenging for children to remember more than that. Once everyone has said their name, throw a ball to a child and say that child's name. The child who catches the ball continues the game. To make the game more challenging, introduce a speed factor.

3. 'Find someone who ...' bingo game

Prepare a bingo card with a short 'Find someone who ...' instruction for each square, for example, 'Find someone who has a pet' (see Appendix, p141). Make sure that you include an instruction which you think only applies to you so that you encourage the children to interact with you from the very beginning. Hand out the cards to the children. Encourage the children to mingle and speak to each other to find a different name to write in each square. When they have a vertical or horizontal line they should shout out, 'Bingo!' Follow up the activity with a chat about the things they have discovered about each other.

4. Spin the bottle

Get the children to sit in a circle with a bottle in the middle. Fill it with a small amount of sand to give it some weight. Spin the bottle. When it stops, establish which student it is pointing to. Find out their name and ask them a simple question such as 'What's your favourite colour?' Continue the game by inviting that child to spin the bottle and ask the next question.

5. Something you don't know about me

Give each student a slip of paper. On it, they write their name and something about themselves that nobody knows yet (for example, a place they have been to or something they like doing). Collect and mix the slips of paper. Then choose one of the slips. Pick three students, one of whom must be the child who wrote the fact you have chosen. The three children stand outside the classroom and read the slip. They prepare their 'claim' to the secret. When they come back in, the class should ask each of the three children three questions to discover who the true owner of the fact is.

6. Snowball fight

Give each child a sheet of recycled paper. They write their names and five things about themselves on it and scrunch it up into a paper snowball. Divide the class into two teams and organise them so that they are standing facing each other at opposite ends of the classroom. When you shout 'Snowball fight!', the children throw their snowballs at each other. Each child picks up or catches a snowball and goes up to the originator. The 'finder' of the snowball presents their new friend to the class with the information they have discovered.

7. Find your sticker friend

A variation to the activity above is to give each child a sticker as they walk into class. Make sure that you have enough matching pairs of stickers for all your students. Play some music and get the children to find their matching 'sticker friend'. Have prompts on the board to help the children interview and present their partner to the class.

8. My special box

Bring a cardboard box into class containing objects and photos that mean something to you. Show the children one item at a time and answer any questions the children may have. Follow the activity up by getting the children to make special boxes of their own, which they can present in a show-and-tell session (see Unit 19).

9. 'This is me' worksheet

This is a great activity for children who don't know how to write yet. Give the children a worksheet entitled 'This is me!' The children write their name and draw some of their favourite things on it. Put up the children's pictures in an exhibition corner and encourage the children to visit each other's profiles.

10. Make a 'class rules' poster

Classroom management starts on day one. Involve the children in the goings-on of the class by getting them to think about how they would like to work and learn together. Start with a discussion about what the behaviour rules should be for both the teacher and the student, so that learning English is fun for everyone. Then create a poster with five rules that everyone agrees on, which the children can help you make and decorate. (For more on managing learners' behaviour, see Units 11 and 12.)

'I prepare a dot-to-dot for each learner where they connect the dots to reveal their name. In the following lessons they can add to it with pictures, stickers or simply rewrite their name with different colours.'

Jennie Wright, teacher and author, Germany

10 ways to approach behaviour in the young learner classroom

Unit 11

Behaviour is a tricky issue in every classroom as it can make or break any lesson. The secret to keeping things under control is to approach behaviour management calmly and logically in order to avoid getting into emotional wars. Here are 10 behaviour management secrets that you may want to try.

1. Don't take behaviour personally

The first secret to managing behaviour is not to take it personally. Remember that the children are simply being children. Don't forget that they will tend to mirror the behaviour and reactions that you have in class, so make sure that you always provide them with a positive role model to follow. Similarly, when telling children why their behaviour is not appropriate, explain that you are not against them, but rather the inappropriate behaviour, which you cannot accept.

2. Encourage the right choices

Always present behaviour management as a choice that the children can make and then hold them accountable for their choices by kindly explaining the situation, eg 'Anya, when you choose to behave like that, you also choose to leave the game. If you change the way you are behaving and respect turn-taking, you will also choose to continue playing the game with us. So, what do you choose to do?'

3. Be consistent and coherent

Before you start the school year, take some time to think about the rules and the type of behaviour that you find unacceptable. Then, calmly think about the consequences for less appropriate behaviour. Make sure that you discuss and agree upon different levels of consequences to match the severity and recurrence of inappropriate behaviour with the children: oral reprimand; time out; note home; class expulsion, visit to the principal's office, etc.

4. Rules poster

Involve the children in making a poster displaying 3–5 behaviour rules and make sure that they understand why each rule exists. Include rules related to topics like class noise, class materials, learning attitude, respect, etc. Once the behaviour for a rule is automatic, substitute that rule with another that still needs working on. Make sure that you follow a 'we' model when making rules, for example, 'When we want to participate, we always put our hands up'. Include general headings before each rule to aid understanding: Noise volume; Participation; Asking for Permission; Respecting and listening to others; Books and materials.

5. Establish a positive classroom environment

Get to know the children as individuals and not just as students. Learn their names as soon as you can by asking them to make personalised name cards (see Unit 6). As you learn more about each child, you will slowly be able to earn their trust and have a personal and meaningful conversation with them.

6. Create a seating plan

Creating a seating plan for each class will have a double effect: first, it will help you manage the class noise level and second, it will help you identify the children and learn their names quickly and efficiently so that you can quickly get their attention and avoid undesirable behaviour. See the Appendix for a sample seating plan (p142).

7. Create routines

Routines are fundamental in any classroom as they show the children what you expect of them and make them feel safe. There are many routines that you can choose from: routines for the beginning and end of a lesson, routines for going to the toilet, routines for packing up, etc.

8. Keep the children busy, focused and on track

Get the children busy from the minute they arrive. Have instructions on the board for them to follow as they walk into class. Train them to read the instructions and get on with their work. Write visual reminders of all tasks on the board in case they get lost during the lesson so that they can avoid unnecessary interruptions.

9. Keep moving

Avoid standing still in one place for too long. Instead, move around the classroom and use your physical presence to encourage the children to stay focused and on track throughout the entire lesson.

10. Positive reinforcement

Instead of focusing on students who are misbehaving, shift your focus and pay most attention to the children who are behaving well, by saying things like, 'Class, look at Deepak! Look how neat his desk is and how his hand is up, waiting patiently for his turn!'

'To avoid misbehaviour in the classroom I always try to keep them busy, choosing challenging and stimulating tasks. If they are too loud after playing a game, for example, I use a bell or a rattle to attract their attention or change the activity.'

Magda Dygała, teacher and trainer, Poland

Unit 11

10 tools for managing behaviour in the young learner classroom

Now that we have discussed 10 secrets to approaching behaviour, let's have a look at 10 valuable tools that can make all the difference when it comes to applying the principles in Unit 11 to your classroom and making behaviour management an objective for everyone in your classroom.

1. Rules and consequences posters

To help children realise that good behaviour is a choice, display a consequences poster next to your rules poster (Unit 11, point 4). The consequences poster lists the outcome of ignoring each rule (eg loss of a privilege, time out, verbal warning, written warning home, phone call to parents, etc.). Refer to these charts regularly so that the children realise that they will be enforced consistently in class.

2. Behaviour chart

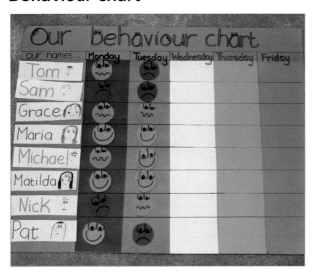

A behaviour chart is an absolute must in every classroom. Filling it in every day can be time-consuming, so make sure you choose a simple weekly write-on, wipe-off behaviour chart with a space for the children to write their names and a square for each lesson so that the children can evaluate their own behaviour with a smiley face at the end of each lesson. This will help to train them to be accountable for their behaviour and to start to develop self-evaluation skills. Remember to choose a student to clean the chart at the end of each week.

3. Responsibility and activity cards

Involve the children in class management by giving them special jobs to do. Have a card on the end of a lanyard that the children can wear as they perform their task of the day. Allocate a timekeeper, a noise controller, a calendar/weather chart keeper, a teacher's assistant to help you hand out and collect things and an attention grabber who can shake a tambourine to help you get the children's attention. Remember to make sure that the jobs rotate so that every child gets a chance to do the different tasks and realise that behaviour management isn't the sole responsibility of the teacher.

4. Noise traffic light and hotel bell

Rather than reprimand children for making noise, try to avoid the problem before it happens. Display a 'noise traffic light' next to the board to help you show the children if the noise they are making is appropriate to the task they are working on or not. If the noise level is perfect, stick a visual cue on the green traffic light. If the class is getting rowdy, ring your hotel bell once to get the children's attention and stick the visual reminder on the yellow light. If the noise level is too high, ring the bell twice, stick the visual reminder on the red light and give the children an opportunity to choose to change their behaviour before you apply a consequence.

 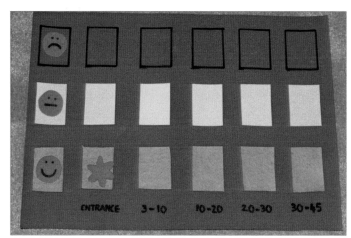

5. Lesson schedule

A lesson can seem never-ending for some children. To lessen this effect, put up a lesson schedule on the board. Divide the board into slots for the main activities of the lesson and write the expected learning time next to them. Then, as you do each activity together, get a child to come up and put a tick next to it. This will help the children get a sense of time and progression.

6. Fast finishers' fun and games box

In some cases, children start misbehaving because they don't have anything to do. Make sure you avoid this by creating a fast finishers' fun activity box. The idea is to give the children something fun and engaging to do once they have finished an allocated task. Include things like crosswords, wordsearches, vocabulary games, spot the difference, etc.

7. Lolly sticks for choosing volunteers

Choosing volunteers in class can be tricky. Sometimes too many children want to do a particular task, and other times the opposite is the case and you practically have to get down on your knees and beg the children to volunteer. Using lolly sticks will help you avoid these situations. Ask the children to bring a lolly stick to class. They write their name on it and decorate it as they wish. Then, put all the sticks in an opaque bag. When you want a volunteer, simply draw a stick out of the bag.

Unit 12

8. Rewards and PAT (Preferred Activity Time)

Positive reinforcement also plays an important role in behaviour management. Make sure you set up a reward system to help you reward good behaviour and boost the children's self-esteem. Include things like stamps, stickers, stars and small treats in your behaviour toolkit. Another option is to reward good behaviour with a PAT activity. Introduce a points system for good behaviour. When the children reach the target, allow them to choose a PAT activity.

9. Behaviour passport

Make a behaviour passport for each child in which you can stamp good behaviour visas. Classroom stamp sets are available online. Include different types of visa pages in your passport: a sharing visa, a tolerance visa, a turn-taking visa, etc. Share the passport with the children's parents and involve them in setting up rewards for their child's good behaviour. See the Appendix for a template (p143).

10. Student behaviour contracts and warning slips – letters to parents

Once you have discussed and set up your classroom rules and behaviour management system, draw up a behaviour contract for each child, which they have to sign and take ownership of. Send a copy home to share with the child's parents and make them aware of your class behaviour policy.

10 routines for the young learner classroom

Routines help us to avoid behaviour problems and save valuable teaching and learning time by encouraging the children to become autonomous. In addition, they make children feel safe and get them into learning mode. However, routines have to be taught and practised over and over again before they become automatic. Here is a list of 10 routines that you can introduce in your classroom.

1. Getting the children into a learning frame of mind

Get the children ready for learning before the lesson begins. Display a 'Good morning' chart outside your classroom to tell children what you want them to do as soon as they enter the classroom. Use topics and key words on your chart to make sure that it's clear and easy to understand.

2. Filling in classroom charts

After the children have entered the classroom, taken off their coats and put their bags away, get them to fill in the attendance chart with their 'avatar'. To create these at the beginning of term, give each child a blank cardboard cut-out of a boy or girl to decorate and write their name on (see Appendix, p144). Each day when they arrive, they put their avatar on the 'At school' section of the chart. Remember to get a helper to put all the avatars back in the 'At home' section at the end of every lesson. Another possibility is to get the children to fill in a calendar and weather chart (see Unit 17, point 6). These charts are great for introducing language in a communicative context.

3. Dealing with personal items

Develop the children's sense of personal responsibility by teaching them how to take the initiative and look after their personal items. Hang up visual reminders in the classroom to remind them what their responsibilities are. Label the children's hooks or cubby holes with name cards in alphabetical order.

4. Singing a song

A song can be a very effective tool to signal a change of activity to children. Try using a hello song to start your lesson, a tidy-up song to signal the end of an activity and a goodbye song to end your lesson. See Units 20–25 for more suggestions.

Unit 13

5. Picking up homework from the homework box

To make sure that every child knows what the homework is, copy the instructions onto a slip of paper for each child. Put the slips in a homework box. At the end of the lesson, each child takes a homework slip from the homework box. This will develop their responsibility, independence and organisation skills.

6. Choosing the teacher's helper for the day

Implement a fair system to choose a teacher's helper each day. Get the children to decorate a peg with their name on it. Hang the pegs on a piece of string. The first peg on the string is the teacher's helper. Once a child has been the teacher's helper, move the peg on the end of the string so that every child gets the chance to be a teacher's helper.

7. Asking for permission

Implement a system in which you reduce the learning time children waste every day asking you for permission to go to the toilet or sharpen their pencils. Make a bathroom pass card for the boys and another for the girls. Hang the passes up next to the door. A child can go to the toilet if there is a pass available. You can also make pencil-sharpening passes that are hung next to the bin.

8. Getting the children's attention

Avoid shouting to get the children's attention. Instead, use a silent gesture like folding your arms and waiting patiently for the children to notice you, or clapping out a rhythm which the children echo back to you. Another option is to use a chant which the children respond to. See Unit 23 for more suggestions.

9. Forming groups

Organising groups can be a time-consuming activity. Reduce time spent on this by preparing a groupwork poster, which you display on the door before the lesson begins. As the children walk into the classroom, they see which group they belong to and automatically join it. Remember to give each group a name or a colour to make it easily identifiable.

10. Getting children's feedback

End the lesson with a quick circle time discussion in which you get the children to think back over the activities they did during the lesson and to choose their favourite one. This feedback will help you plan your future lessons in a motivating and engaging way. For an example feedback form, see Appendix, page 146.

Unit 13

10 thoughts on instructions

Instructions can make or break a lesson. If children understand what you want them to do, they will be able to meet your expectations and the lesson will run smoothly. However, if instructions are confusing, chaos and confusion may ensue, requiring a lot of your time and effort to get things back under control. See Appendix (p147) for some common and useful classroom instructions for use in particular situations. To get some ideas on how to give effective instructions, have a look at the 10 tips below.

1. Plan instructions

Instructions are fundamental in the classroom, so spend time carefully planning the instructions that you give. As you plan the activities for your lesson, think of and plan the corresponding instructions that you will need for a particular activity. This may initially appear time-consuming, but it will save you and the children a lot of stress in the classroom. See the Appendix for a list of useful classroom instructions (p147).

2. Keep instructions short and simple

Keep your instructions short, simple and to the point. Remember that children have a short attention span and are eager to get going on a task. So, if your instructions are long and complicated, they are likely to switch off or forget everything that you have said, even before they start doing anything.

3. Word instructions positively

Make sure that your instructions tell the children what you want them to do rather than what you don't want them to do. They should be in the affirmative form. For example, instead of saying, 'Don't shout!', try saying, 'Speak quietly – use volume 5.' (You will have to have agreed on what volume 5 is with the children.)

4. Sequence instructions

Give instructions in a sequenced manner. Follow a 1-2-3 approach to giving instructions: First open your books, then read the story, and finally do Exercise 1. Write this on the board in three steps, numbered 1, 2 and 3, so that the children can go back to the instructions if they forget them as they become immersed in the activity.

5. Repeat instructions

Make sure you give instructions more than once. Children have different learning rhythms and language levels, which will mean that they don't all understand you at the same time. Some children may need to hear an instruction several times before they understand what you want them to do.

6. Demonstrate instructions

Remember that young learners still have a very basic command of English. To avoid misunderstandings, give children instructions while demonstrating exactly what you want them to do. Think of yourself as a mirror, constantly reflecting what you want the children to do.

7. Check understanding

Once you have given an instruction, take the time to check whether the children have understood. Don't limit yourself to asking, 'Do you understand?' The natural answer to this question tends to be 'Yes'. Try getting the children to repeat the instruction back to you like a parrot or in a parrot voice. This will allow them to have fun and stay on track at the same time.

8. Give instructions in English

Avoid using the children's first language to give instructions. Instructions are a natural and communicative opportunity for children to pick up and learn new language. Remember that children need as much exposure to English as they can get.

9. Make instructions visual

Children respond well to visual stimuli. This means that they tend to remember what they see rather than what they hear or are told to do. Make cards with an instruction and an illustrative image on each. Show the children these cards as you give them the instructions.

10. Give instructions on a need-to-know basis

Avoid bombarding children with a long list of instructions. By the time you get to the end, they will probably have forgotten what you wanted them to do first. Instead, give them instructions for a particular activity on a need-to-know basis. This means that the children are given time to complete each task before being given the next instruction.

'I always try to keep instructions simple, use short and clear sentences and support my instructions with pictures, gestures, intonation or even miming. I make sure everyone understands them by asking simple questions.'

Rosa Maria Figueiroa, Spain

10 ways to start and end lessons

The way you start and end a lesson is important. At the beginning of the lesson, you need to warm the children up for what they are about to learn, and at the end, you need to give them 'closure' on what they have learned. The first five activities are warmers to help you start your lessons effectively. Activities 6–10 are coolers; these will help you bring your lesson to a close.

1. Meet and greet at the door

Treat the children like guests that are visiting your home and meet and greet them at the classroom door. This will help you bond with the children and show them that you care about them. You can also end your lesson by saying goodbye to each child at the door. When you do this, try saying something positive about what each child has done in that particular lesson, for example, 'Maria, I really liked the way you pronounced 'teacher' today! What a star you are!' Make sure that the feedback you give is genuine.

2. Define learning objectives

Start your lesson by giving the children a learning map of what is going to happen in that lesson. Define and discuss 3–5 learning objectives with the children for that lesson, for example, 'Today we are going to learn eight new words about farm animals. We are also going to learn how to say these words properly in English. Then we are going to write a sentence about our favourite farm animal and illustrate it.' Write these objectives in the top right-hand corner of the board. Come back to them throughout the lesson and tick them off as you achieve them. This will give the children a sense of progression of the lesson and allow them to see how well they are learning in your class.

3. Sing a familiar song or say a chant

You can signal to the children that your lesson has begun by singing a familiar song or getting them to say a routine chant. For examples of chants that you can use, see Unit 23. To make the activity more challenging, try getting the children to say it faster and faster each time or to repeat it using a different voice, for example, 'This time, let's say our chant in a happy voice.' Good voices to use are ones showing different emotions such as happy, sad, hungry, tired, disappointed, or character voices, for example, a princess, a dragon, a witch or a monster.

4. Challenge of the day

Start your lesson by writing a riddle on the board for the children to solve. An example might be, 'What has a face and two hands but no arms or legs?' (Answer: a clock.) This will challenge children from the minute they walk through the door. As the children get better at solving these challenges, they can come up with their own for the class to solve next time. For more ideas, see Appendix, p149.

5. Five minutes of quiet reading time

If you are teaching after PE or break time, for example, you will often need to calm the children down before you start working with them. A good strategy is to take in some picture books. Invite the children to choose one and read it quietly for five minutes. After the allotted time, everyone will have calmed down and you can begin your lesson.

ETpedia: Young Learners © Pavilion Publishing and Media Ltd and its licensors 2016.

Unit 15

6. Revision activity: quiz game

A fun way to end your lesson is to get the children to play a game that encourages them to remember and practise what they have learned. Jeopardy (see Appendix, p150) is a quiz game in which the children pick a box and answer a question in order to win the amount of money displayed on the box. The lower the value, the easier the question. The winner is the player/team with the most money at the end.

7. 'What have you learned today?' discussion

Children love puppets. A fun way to end the lesson is to get the children to sit in a big circle and to encourage them to tell the class puppet what they can remember about that lesson. You can help them by referring back to the lesson objectives on the board. This is also a great way of finding out what your children enjoyed and getting feedback about your lesson.

8. Self-evaluation

If you have a behaviour and learning chart, you can get the children to go up to these charts at the end of the lesson after they have packed up and fill them in by drawing smiley faces on them. See the appendix for a personalised self-evaluation chart that children can fill at their desk.

9. Goodbye song

You can end your lesson with a routine that involves singing a familiar goodbye song, for example:

Goodbye, Goodbye	Goodbye, Goodbye
It's time to go!	See you soon!
Hurry up, Hurry up,	Goodbye, Goodbye
It's time to tidy up	See you soon!

There are countless songs to choose from on YouTube. Remember to choose one that is simple and repetitive so that it's quick and easy to learn.

10. Awards ceremony

End on a high by having a short awards ceremony at the end of the lesson. You could give rewards for the hardest worker, the most helpful student or the neatest handwriting. The winner can wear a badge or be the teacher's helper in the next lesson.

10 ways to use stirrers and settlers

Children have a short attention span, so it's important to make sure that you monitor their energy in the classroom to prevent them from getting too excited or too bored. To keep them focused and on track, make sure that the activities you choose are short, and that you pace your lesson well by including various stirrers and settlers in your plan. **Stirrers** are activities that are designed to get children excited and allow them to use up their energy by getting them to move around. **Settlers** have the opposite effect. They are designed to get children to calm down after a stirrer and into a quieter frame of mind for the next activity. Below is a list of 10 stirrers and settlers that you can try out in your classroom.

1. Play a ball game

This is a stirrer in which the children play a game that helps them practise target language and move around. A simple idea is to play a ball game. Introduce a vocabulary topic, eg clothes. The children stand in a circle and throw a ball to each other. The child who catches the ball has to say a word belonging to that particular word set, eg 'skirt'. To adapt the activity for weaker learners, allow them to repeat the words that they've heard.

2. Play a flashcard mingling game

Choose a topic. Distribute a set of flashcards or word cards related to that topic to the children. Each child then sticks their flashcard or word card on another child's back without that child seeing what is on it. The children then move around the room asking each other questions to guess who they are. For more flashcard game ideas, see Units 35 and 36.

3. Conduct a survey

Invite the children to move around the room conducting a class survey (see Appendix, p152) relating to a topic that you are teaching, for example, 'What's your favourite food?' Then get the children to make a pie chart poster with their survey results.

4. Sing a song or chant

Start singing a song or chant that the children have already learned, for example, 'If you're happy and you know it'. Then sing it faster and faster to stir things up. The children will soon be out of breath and ready for your next activity.

5. Do a drama activity

The children roleplay a simple dialogue for the class. Begin by writing a simple dialogue on the board with the children. Drill it with the class by getting them to repeat it various times. Then, the children repeat the dialogue using an emotion (eg happy, angry, bored, frustrated) in pairs. Finally, invite the children to add gestures to their dialogue and roleplay it for the class. For added fun, have a box of realia and old clothes that they can use, or get the children to make simple paper-plate masks.

6. Use a routine activity

This activity works well as a settler. Help the children to calm down by triggering a familiar routine that the children are used to. You could sing a song they already know or do a simple yoga breathing exercise.

ETpedia: Young Learners © Pavilion Publishing and Media Ltd and its licensors 2016.

Unit 16

7. Play sorting games

Try a categorising activity in which you give the class 12 random words they have already learned, which they have to organise into lexical sets. To begin with, give the children the lexical set categories to guide them. As they become used to this type of exercise, encourage them to come up with the categories themselves.

8. Read and draw

Read out a short, simple descriptive text and get the children to draw a picture of what they hear. Once they have drawn their pictures, follow up the activity by getting them to write one or two short sentences about their picture. (See the Appendix for sample texts, p153.)

9. Alternate your lesson activities with a story

Give the children some time out by reading them a story between activities. With larger classes, photocopy and enlarge the main images of the story and put them up on the board as you read.

10. Plan for individual activity time

Remember that we all like a breather every now and then, so plan a quiet moment in every lesson when the children can stop and read a book or do a simple arts and crafts activity. For more ideas on this, see Units 31 and 32.

'Stirrers and settlers such as games, puzzles and songs create interest and excitement and have a positive effect on the young learner's behaviour.'

Renal Bakr, English teacher, Egypt

10 key resources for your teacher toolkit

As teachers, we have to be ready for anything that may happen during a lesson. This inevitably means that we need to be flexible and adapt our lesson plan, whenever necessary, to meet our students' needs. A well-equipped tool kit will help us do that. Here are 10 key resources to help you stock up.

1. Flashcards/word cards, posters, realia

Flashcards help to make learning visual, and make the meaning clear for learners. They also allow them to have fun and play games to drill new vocabulary. So make sure you have a complete set. You may also want to include a set of corresponding word cards and a few posters too. Don't forget to take along some poster tack or magnets to put everything up on the board. An alternative to flashcards is realia, which is perfect for drama activities or games.

2. 'Classroom language' cards

A set of 'classroom language' cards will also save you time and help avoid confusion in the classroom. They will help you give instructions in English and expose children to language in context, which they will soon pick up. The following signs are useful: 'Quiet', 'Time to clean up', 'Look and Listen', 'Please raise your hand' and 'Please line up'.

3. Noise maker

A noise maker, like a tambourine or a bell, will help the children realise that you need them to focus and have their eyes on you. This will save you raising your voice.

4. Puppets

Puppets transport children to imaginary worlds. They also encourage shy children to speak up by giving them a 'crutch'. Additionally, they can be a classroom management tool by whispering secrets like 'I'm getting earache. It's too noisy!' to you. A set of finger puppets of the main characters in your coursebook will help the children practise speaking skills by roleplaying the stories and dialogues they read.

5. Arts and crafts materials

Make sure that your teacher kit has lots of plain white and coloured paper, pens, crayons and markers, and perhaps some modelling clay for children to make their own learning materials or a bingo card to fill up those extra five minutes that you hadn't planned for.

6. Calendar and weather chart

A calendar and weather chart is a great way to help you start your lesson. It gives the children the opportunity to record the day's weather and date and any important event, such as a school trip or a birthday. It allows children to revise vocabulary such as the days of the week, months of the year, numbers and the weather, as well as structures like 'What's the date today?' 'What's the weather like today?' 'What day was it yesterday?' 'What day is it tomorrow?' in context.

7. Mini-whiteboards

A cheap set of mini-whiteboards is an invaluable tool in your teacher kit. Ideally, have one per child to play spelling games, 'Identify the flashcard' games, 'What's the odd word out?', etc., which help you see evidence of learning for each child.

8. A games kit

Children love games, so no teacher should be without a games kit. Make sure that you have a dice and some counters (at least one set per group) to play board games. It's also useful to have a big class copy of games that can be adapted to any unit you are teaching, for example, a set of bingo cards, a big noughts-and-crosses card or a giant Jeopardy board (see Unit 15, point 6).

9. Letter formation worksheets

If you are teaching younger learners or learners whose first language does not follow the Latin alphabet, this is a tool that will make your and their lives much easier. Remember to include a set of handwriting/letter formation worksheets for less advanced students and one for more advanced students. Although most coursebooks have some handwriting letter formation practice, this is usually not enough to get every child to develop their writing skills to the point that they can write quickly and confidently. See the Appendix for sample letter formation worksheets.

10. Teacher diary

It is important to have a little something for yourself, too; something that will help you reflect on your teaching practice so that you can rise to the occasion and make a difference. This is why you need a teacher diary or blog to record the most important things that happen in class so that you can reflect on them calmly and critically afterwards. It is useful for you to write about what didn't go as well as you hoped, but it is just as important to write about what went well, so that in future, you can include activities in your lesson plan which appeal to the characteristics and needs of the children you are teaching. See Unit 50 for some links to teacher blogs.

Unit 17

10 situations in which to use classroom language

Speaking English in class is a great opportunity to expose children to English in a clear, communicative context. As they hear the language again and again, they soon start to pick it up and use it naturally. As teachers, we often spend hours planning, but forget to think about the language that we'll use to speak to the children. Here are 10 learning situations and suggested corresponding classroom language to get the children listening to and responding in English in class every day.

1. Preparing to start a lesson

It is important to get the children into an English frame of mind from the beginning of the lesson. You can use the first few minutes of your lesson to speak to children and say things like: 'Welcome back to school! How was your holiday? Did you have fun?' 'Hi, How are you today?' 'So, what did you do yesterday/over the weekend?' 'Who remembers what we worked on yesterday?' 'Can anyone remember what we did yesterday?' 'What did we do last lesson?' 'What was your homework?' 'Take out your homework/books/tablets please!' 'Please hand in your homework!' 'Please put your homework on the homework pile!' 'Is anyone absent today?' 'Who is absent today?'

2. Working on the board

The way that you manage your board is important, but the language that you use to speak about what is happening on the board is just as crucial: '1-2-3: eyes and ears on the board, please!' 'Look at the board now, please!' 'Come to the board, please', 'Stick the correct flashcard on the board!' 'Clean the board, please!' 'Copy down the words on the board in your notebooks carefully, please!'

3. Correcting homework

Homework is an important way for children to reflect on and practise what they have done in class. It's also important that they know if they have made any mistakes. The following classroom language will help you correct homework in class in English: 'What is the answer to exercise two?' 'Who wants to correct question one?' 'Marta, can you please give us your answer for question one?'

4. Playing games

Children love playing games. Make sure that the language you use is short and clear as children will naturally be excited and impatient at this stage of the lesson: 'Let's play a game!' 'Can you remember the rules for this game?' 'Look carefully and try to remember what's missing!' 'The first team to … gets a point.' 'That's right, this team gets a point.' 'It's your turn now!' 'It's your turn to throw the dice.' 'Please shuffle the cards.' 'Sorry, try again!'

5. Checking instructions

If you give an instruction or explanation and ask the children if they have understood, they are likely to answer 'yes', regardless of whether they actually have. Instead, try saying: 'Now who can remind us of what we need to do?' 'So, what are we doing again?' 'Lisa, can you please repeat what we are going to do?' 'Can anyone repeat my instructions?' 'Are we going to … or are we going to …?'

ETpedia: Young Learners © Pavilion Publishing and Media Ltd and its licensors 2016.

6. Checking understanding

As you go through your lesson, remember to stop every now and again and check that the children are still on board by saying things like: 'Please put up your hand if you know the answer to this question.' 'Is this a picture of a … or a …?' 'How do you ask someone to … in English?' 'Show me a …' 'Point to a …' 'Where is the …?'

7. Promoting critical thinking

As teachers, we spend a lot of time in class making sure that children know the right answers to questions, but we also need to make sure that the class understands the thinking that leads to the right answer. After correcting a question, remember to ask a follow-up question like 'What makes you say that?' 'How do you know that?' 'Why do you say/think that?' 'Can you explain how you know that is the correct answer?'

8. Giving feedback

Remember to reward hard work with feedback and praise by saying things like: 'Well done!' 'That's fantastic!' 'What a star!' 'What hard work!' 'I'm so proud of you!' 'This is really looking much better.' 'I'm so proud that you tried again.' 'There's a tiny mistake there. Please look carefully and try again.'

9. Practising pronunciation

It's important that children learn to pronounce language correctly. Make children aware of the correct pronunciation by saying: 'Repeat after me, please!' 'Say this again more slowly/quickly, please!' 'Repeat the whole sentence, please!' 'Now, you try saying it.' 'How do you say this word?' 'Where's the stress in this word?'

10. Ending the lesson

We often close our lessons with an end-of-lesson routine. The language that we use should also become routine for the children, so remember to say things like: 'Tick, tock, tick, tock, it's time to pack up!' 'Put your books away!' 'Please collect your notebooks.' 'Please put your work on my desk.' 'Great job, everyone!' 'See you next lesson.' 'Goodbye! See you next time!' 'Thank you for your hard work, everyone!' 'Bye bye!'

Unit 18

10 reasons and tips for doing show and tell

'Show and tell' is a great activity for developing children's communication and public speaking skills. It involves a child bringing an item of their choice into school and presenting it to the class for a few minutes. Points 1–5 below are aimed at giving you reasons to introduce show-and-tell activities in your classroom. Points 6–10 are intended to provide you with useful tips to make sure that your show-and-tell activities run smoothly and develop the children's communication skills.

1. Train speaking stamina

Show and tell is a great speaking activity to develop the children's speaking stamina, as they are challenged to speak about something that is meaningful to them. Since the children are emotionally attached to the topic they are speaking about, they are naturally engaged in the activity and are able to train their speaking skills in a safe, stress-free environment.

2. Build their public speaking skills

Another reason to use show and tell is that it challenges and trains the children to speak in public in front of their peers. Being a confident and efficient public speaker is a crucial skill to learn, as most jobs nowadays involve sharing information with other people. The more accustomed children are to doing this as a matter of course, the better.

3. Make learning personal

Show and tell has the clear advantage of encouraging the children to apply language they are learning in class to their everyday lives in an authentic and naturally communicative context. This is empowering for children, as they soon realise that they can use English to speak about themselves and the things that matter most to them.

4. Find out more about each student

This speaking activity also provides you with the ideal opportunity to get to know each child in your class better, as it gives you a chance to find out more about a child's personal life, likes and interests. As a result, you will soon be able to establish a meaningful relationship with the children in your classroom.

5. Provide a sense of progress

This activity is both teacher- and student-friendly as it allows you to evaluate each child's speaking skills while giving them a clear sense of progression and achievement. As the child's peers ask follow-up questions and provide feedback, the child learns that the harder they work and prepare, the more effective and engaging their presentation will be.

6. Topics for show and tell

There is only one basic rule when it comes to choosing topics for a show-and-tell activity: the child should be able to relate the topic to their personal life and experience. Start with topics like: My family, My favourite toy, My pet, My house, My favourite sport, etc.

7. Scaffold the task

In order to make sure that children are not put on the spot during a show-and-tell presentation, make sure that you walk them through the process of preparing their show-and-tell 'speech'. Start by teaching them to brainstorm the topic as a class, and then to think about which approach they want to follow and how they are going to prepare for the big moment. Make sure that you give them the opportunity to practise giving their talk to a peer before asking them to share their work with the group. This will greatly reduce the pressure that children experience.

8. Encourage follow-up questions

Explain to the children that show and tell is all about listening to and sharing experiences. Encourage the children to think of and ask follow-up questions that they are genuinely interested in after a show-and-tell presentation. This may be the perfect opportunity for the children to find a soulmate who has the same interests as they do.

9. Do it on a set day

Make show and tell a habit in your classroom by doing it at a set time on a set day. This is a good activity to use when children are tired, namely, during the last lesson of the week. The fact that the children are speaking about something meaningful to them will motivate them to go the extra mile.

10. Use a 'crutch' for shy students

Some children are terrified by the idea of speaking in public. Help shy children deal with their fear by giving them a crutch that they can lean on when speaking in public. This could be a puppet, a slide presentation or even a video recording of their presentation.

'Praise and reward students. It creates a positive atmosphere and reminds students of your expectations.'

Emma Johnston, teacher, International House Toruń

Unit 19

Songs, chants and rhymes

Songs, chants and rhymes are an excellent way of developing children's speaking and pronunciation skills. This section will begin by analysing why teaching songs, chants and rhymes is so beneficial for young learners.

Units 21–23 will provide you with tried-and-tested suggestions of songs, chants and activities to take into the young learner classroom that will simultaneously appeal to children's interests and needs, and help them learn and speak English naturally and in context.

Units 24 and 25 will focus on silly tongue twisters and fun rhymes that help you work on and improve the children's pronunciation skills without their realising that they are working hard.

10 reasons to use songs and chants in the young learner classroom

Two essential tools for a teacher of young learners are songs and chants which relate to the different topics that you are teaching. Songs and chants are also very versatile classroom management tools, which you can use as warmers, transition markers or coolers to meet your teaching objectives for a particular lesson. Here is a list of 10 reasons to use songs and chants in your classroom.

1. A regular rhythm

Songs and chants have a regular rhythm which is almost repetitive and intuitive. This is a fantastic way for you to work on teaching children pronunciation and intonation in English without boring them to sleep. Once children have learned the rhythm of a song, all they have to do is to slot in the language. This is a fun way of helping them distance themselves from first language influences.

2. Catchy

A good song or chant can stick in our ears and memories for a whole day. This means that when children learn a new song or chant, they will be picking up and practising language without even realising it.

3. Language in context

Songs and chants present children with a clear context in which they can use the language they are learning and encourage children to apply and use this language in other contexts.

4. Confidence-building

Songs and chants are a great way to get shy children to speak in class. Singing a song or saying a chant as a whole class allows shy students to join in a speaking activity without feeling exposed in front of the class. They are also presented with the opportunity of repeating the target language over and over until they have mastered it. This means that when you do ask them to sing or speak on their own, they will be able to do it well because of all the practice they have had. Consequently, their confidence and motivation will be enhanced.

5. Memory and concentration

We have already focused on the fact that songs and chants are repetitive and that they allow children to repeat the target language over and over until they are able to sing the song or say the chant on their own. This natural repetition allows children to develop their memory and concentration skills which will be essential language learning tools later on in the learning process.

6. Introducing and ending a topic

Because songs and chants are fun, they are a fantastic way of introducing or ending a topic. They can often be easily related to a story or any other activity that you are doing in class. Thus, songs and chants are a great way of complementing coursebook activities.

7. Mixed abilities

We all teach in mixed-ability classrooms in which children have different levels and learning rhythms. Many children learn best when they see and hear the target language that we are teaching them; adding an element of movement is also important for a lot of younger learners. Songs have the added advantage of being available online, often with videos that we can use to motivate children to learn the target language.

8. Variety of skills

Another great reason to use songs and chants in the young learner language classroom is that they allow children to work on various skills in one activity. Children develop their listening skills as they first hear and learn a particular song or chant. As they are learning it, they are automatically working on their speaking skills. You can easily develop writing skills by getting children to write a short sentence or text about the song or chant they have leant.

9. Cross curricular

Many schools across the globe have adopted a 'CLIL' (Content and Language Integrated Language Learning) approach to teaching English. This means that children are learning important subject content related to subjects such as geography, history, the arts, maths and science in English. Songs and chants are a natural, fun and easy way of encouraging children to learn subject-specific language.

10. Fun

Perhaps the most important reason to use songs and chants in the classroom is the fact that they are fun. Why not spend the last two minutes of a lesson listening to a song for pleasure?

'A good way to help shy singers is to give them finger puppets, or get them to draw a face on their index finger so that the puppet can sing instead.'

Kylie Malinowska, Young Learner Advisor, International House World

Unit 20

10 classics for the young learner classroom

The songs that you use in the classroom need to meet various criteria in order to guarantee that children are having fun and learning language at the same time. A good song needs to be memorable and enjoyable, and should introduce enough target language for the level that you are teaching. Great songs also repeat and drill that target language to a good rhythm, which sticks in children's memories long after your lesson has finished. Here is a list of 10 all-time favourite songs for the young learner classroom. You can find the words in the Appendix (p161) and make copies of them. To get to know the tunes, search for these songs on YouTube.

1. Head, Shoulders, Knees and Toes

This is an active song that gets the children up and out of their seats. It's a perfect one to use when you are teaching the topic of the body, as it drills the following words: head, shoulders, knees, toes, eyes, ears, mouth, nose, feet, tummies, arms, chins, shins, hands, fingers, legs, lips and hips. The children touch each part of the body as they say the word. Speed up the pace as you sing each new verse.

2. The Hokey Cokey

This is another fun song to use when teaching words for parts of the body. Although it drills fewer vocabulary items (right arm, left arm, right leg, left leg and 'whole self'), it does teach children nice chunks of language and the concept of right and left, which they often find difficult. The children stand in a circle and do the actions that they are singing. When they have finished, they all jump into the circle at the same time.

3. The Colours of the Rainbow

Teach the children this song about colours to the tune of The Wheels on the Bus.

Substitute 'red and orange' with 'yellow, green and blue' and 'indigo and violet' the second and third time you sing it.

4. If You're Happy and You Know It

This is a wonderful action song for raising energy levels in the classroom and getting the children into a good mood. It also has the benefit of drilling language chunks relating to action verbs which are perfect for the children to do as they sing the song.

5. Do You Like Broccoli Ice Cream?

If you're looking for a fun song to teach words on the topic of food, you'll love this. It drills vocabulary such as broccoli, ice cream, doughnuts, juice, popcorn, pizza, bananas and soup, as well as the structures children need to talk about their likes and dislikes: 'Do you like …?', 'Yes, I do' and 'No, I don't.' It also surprises children by joining words together that they wouldn't expect to find. Get the children to do a thumbs up and thumbs down action as they sing the song.

6. The Wheels on the Bus

If you want to prepare a little surprise for parents' day or the end-of-year party, try this song, which you can get the children to act out. From a language point of view, it helps children learn onomatopoeic sounds that are associated with words in English: wipers (swish), horn (beep), money (clink), baby (wah) and mummy (shush).

7. Incy Wincy Spider

This is a popular finger rhyme that has survived the test of time. It's a perfect song to use when teaching children about animals or the weather. Get the children to do the actions as they sing.

8. Old Macdonald Had a Farm

If you're looking for a fun onomatopoeic song to teach about animals and the sounds they make, try this. The song drills the following vocabulary: cow (moo), pig (oink), duck (quack), horse (neigh), lamb (baa) and chickens (cluck), and stays in the children's memories long after the lesson has ended. Get the children to imitate the animals as they sing the song.

9. Five Little Monkeys

Children love monkeys and their playful nature. This song allows the children to play as they sing and roleplay the actions they are singing. It is also easy enough for children to sing to their parents in order to show them what they have been learning in class.

10. The Alphabet Song

An alphabet song helps you develop children's literacy skills. This one has been tried and tested in classrooms all over the world for years and can easily be turned into a chant. Get the children to make letter shapes with their fingers as they sing.

'Young learners are very enthusiastic about songs. I always try to choose the ones with built in actions and repetitive lyrics; for example "The Wheels on the Bus" for actions or "The Hokey Cokey" for prepositions of movement. These types of songs help students develop their memory and physical co-ordination as well as build their confidence.'

Magda Dygała, teacher and trainer

10 activities to do with songs and chants

Getting children to learn a new song or chant involves far more than simply getting them to sing or say it a few times. Remember that before children can sing a song or say a chant, they need to learn the melody (in the case of the song) and the rhythm. Start by having them hum the melody and clap to the rhythm a few times. Then, slowly introduce the words and sing the song or say the chant several times. Turn down the volume to find out whether the children are ready to sing or say it on their own. Here is a list of 10 activities that you can do with songs and chants.

1. Guess the words

Before you actually start teaching children the song or chant, share the title with them and let them guess which key words will be in it. Write the words the children guess on the board. With younger learners, stick a flashcard next to each word card to help them identify the words. As they hear the chant, ask the children to stand up each time they hear one of the words on the board.

2. Hold up pictures

Hand out flashcards of the key words in the song or chant to the children at random. Ask these children to hold the flashcards in front of their chests so that everyone can see them. Play the song or chant and ask the children with the flashcards to wave them in the air each time they hear the word on their flashcard. As a follow-up activity, ask the children to put the flashcards on the board in the order they hear them in the song/chant.

3. Point to the flashcard

Show the children flashcards of the key vocabulary in the song or chant. Then play a flashcard game of your choice with them. For flashcard game suggestions, see Units 35 and 36. Once the children know the words, display the flashcards and corresponding word cards around the class. Ask the children to point to the flashcard as they hear the word in the song or chant.

4. Sing in sections

To learn the song or chant, the children will need to sing or say it several times. To prevent this from becoming boring, transform the drilling activity into a fun competition. Choose three children to be the jury. Divide the class into groups. Begin by teaching the whole class a small part of the song or chant. Then divide the class in two and repeat that part of the song or chant with each group. Next, get each group to perform their version to the rest of the class. When the last group has finished, invite the jury to vote for the best group. To speed up the process of grouping children, divide the class into a girls' and boys' team and see which group can sing the best.

5. Invent and mime actions

Once the children know the song, encourage them to take ownership of it by choosing actions that they can do while singing it. They practise the actions several times, then they sing the song and do the gestures together. Film the children and share the video with parents on the school webpage.

6. Sing faster

After the children have sung the song or said the chant a few times, they may start to get bored and lose interest. Keep them focused by introducing a cognitive challenge such as singing the song faster and faster each time. Have a competition to see who can sing the fastest without making a mistake.

7. Fill in the missing gapped words

With older young learners, work on listening for specific language with more formal listening exercises like filling in gaps in the songsheet or listening and circling the correct words. Alternatives to this type of exercise are giving the children 10 statements about the song which they need to classify as true or false, or giving the children sentence halves which they need to listen to and match. Adapt the activity for younger learners by giving them word halves to complete.

8. Invent a verse and roleplay the song or chant

A nice, challenging post-listening activity is to have the class invent the next verse of the song. This activity can be done as a whole class, in groups or in pairs, depending on the characteristics of the class. The children can then prepare a performance of the song to present to parents or to teach to other children in the school. Children often feel empowered when they are asked to teach younger children.

9. Do a class survey and write a song review

This activity focuses on how the children reacted to the song. Two popular options are a class song survey (see Appendix, page 168) or a song review, which can be displayed for everyone to see in the school foyer.

10. Draw the song

Songs appeal to children because of repetitive melodies and the emotions they bring out. They can change our mood on a particular day and put a smile on our face. Make children aware of this by getting them to listen to the song and draw a picture of how it makes them feel. You can then develop writing skills by asking the children to write a sentence about their picture.

Unit 22

10 chants for the young learner classroom

Like songs, chants are a perfect way to get children to learn English in a natural context. They can either be chanted or sung to a tune that the children already know well. Below is a list of 10 types of chant that you can use in your classroom. Chants 1–6 are for classroom management and chants 7–10 relate to topics that are typically covered in the young learner classroom.

1. A chant to signal the start of the lesson

Here is a chant that you can use to signal the beginning of your lesson.

Point to the ceiling

Point to the floor

Point to the window

Point to the door

Stand up

Clap your hands: one [clap], two [clap] three [clap]

Now sit down and look at me.

2. A chant to signal the end of the lesson

This chant signals the end of the lesson and helps revise language.

If you've tidied up, clap your hands [clap, clap]

If you've packed your bag, touch your chin [touch your chin]

If you're listening, touch your head [touch your head]

If you're ready to go, touch your nose [touch your nose].

3. A chant to signal that it's time to tidy up

Here is a chant that you can use to encourage children to tidy up. It is sung to the tune of Twinkle, Twinkle, Little Star.

Twinkle, twinkle, little star

Time to clean up where you are

Put your work back in its place

With a smile upon your face

Twinkle, twinkle, little star

Time to clean up where you are.

4. Chants to get the children's attention

Try using chants that the children must respond to in order to signal that they're listening and ready to start the next activity.

Teacher: One, two, three: eyes on me.

Children: One, two: eyes on you!

5. A chant to signal a transition in the lesson:

Use this chant to show children that you are moving on to the next activity.

5-4-3-2-1

Be in your seat when I am done!

Five! [clap, clap, clap]

Four! [clap, clap, clap]

Three! [clap, clap, clap]

Two! [clap, clap, clap]

One! [clap, clap, clap]

I'm done!

6. A chant to quieten children down

Here's a simple chant that you can use to avoid shouting and quieten the children down.

Put your finger on your lips, on your lips, shh, shh

Put your finger on your lips, on your lips, shh, shh

Put your finger on your lips and don't let it slip

Put your finger on your lips, on your lips, shh, shh.

7. Jazz chants

In her book, *Creating Songs and Chants* (Resource Books for Teachers: Oxford University Press, 2006), Carolyn Graham suggests making up chants according to the number of syllables in a word and then repeating the pattern. This is an easy formula that you can follow for any topic:

Apple, banana, pear

Apple, banana, pear

Apple, banana, apple, banana

Apple, banana, pear.

8. Colour chants

To make chants more fun, get the children to add gestures to the chant like pointing to things around them.

Vr Vr Vr Vroom

Beep, beep, beep

Red and orange

Red and orange

Yellow, blue and green

Yellow, blue and green

Indigooo!!!

And violet too!

Vr Vr Vr Vroom

Beep, beep, beep.

9. A time chant

Do you know what time it is, what time it is, what time it is?

Do you know what time it is?

It's _____ o'clock in the (morning/afternoon).

10. A weather chant

To engage the children, try personalising the chants you use.

Rain, rain, go away! Come again another day.

Rain, rain, go away. Little *[child's name]* wants to play!

10 categories of tongue twister

Tongue twisters are a great way of making children aware of English vowel and consonant sounds. They love repeating these silly sentences or rhymes that practise a particular sound. To make a tongue twister even more challenging, get the children to say it faster and faster each time they repeat it. They will make lots of slips, but have fun in the process. Here is a list of 10 categories with related tongue twisters that you can use in your classroom. The first six are about specific topics, the following three are about celebrations, and the last category is dedicated to tongue twisters traditionally learned by children whose first language is English.

1. The weather

This rhyme practises the sound /w/.

Whether the weather is warm, whether the weather is hot, we have to put up with the weather, whether we like it or not.

2. Food

This silly sentence practises the sound /k/.

Give papa a cup of proper coffee in a copper coffee cup.

This sentence practises the sound /f/.

Fresh fried fish, fish fried fresh, fried fish fresh, fish fried fresh.

This one practises the sound /g/.

Grilled ground beef is good grub.

3. Animals

This silly sentence practises the sound /b/.

A big black bug bit a big black bear on his big black nose.

And this one practises the sounds /f/ and /w/.

Fuzzy wuzzy was a bear. Fuzzy wuzzy had no hair. Fuzzy wuzzy wasn't very fuzzy, was he?

This silly sentence practises the sounds /s/, /l/ and /iː/.

Six silly sheep still asleep.

This one practises the sound /z/.

Zero zebras zig-zagged into the zoo.

4. Colours

This silly sentence practises the sound /ɛ/.

Red lorry, yellow lorry. [x 3]

5. Shopping

This sentence practises the sounds /b/ and /aɪ/.

If you want to buy, buy, if you don't want to buy, bye bye.

6. Summer holidays

This tongue twister practises the sound /s/.

Sally sells sea shells on the sea shore.

This one practises the sounds /aɪ/ and /iː/.

I scream, you scream, we all scream for ice cream.

7. Halloween

This silly sentence practises the sounds /w/, /l/ and /ɒ/.

If two witches were watching two watches, which witch would watch which watch?

And this one practises the sounds /g/ and /ɒ/.

Gobbling gargoyles gobbled gobbling goblins.

8. Christmas

This silly sentence practises the sound /s/.

Seven Santas sang silly songs.

This one practises the sounds /ɛ/ and /iː/.

Eleven elves licked eleven little liquorice lollipops.

9. Easter

This silly sentence practises the sound /b/.

Busy bunnies bring blue baskets.

This one practises the sound /dʒ/.

Jogging jellybeans joke and giggle, jogging jelly beans jump and giggle.

10. Traditional tongue twisters

This tongue twister practises the sound /p/.

Peter Piper picked a peck of pickled peppers. Where's the peck of pickled peppers Peter Piper picked?

This silly rhyme practises the sounds /tʃ/ and /w/.

How much wood would a woodchuck chuck if a woodchuck could chuck wood?

Unit 24

10 fun rhymes to use in the young learner classroom

Rhymes are an effective and motivating tool to use in the young learner classroom as they are very child friendly and simple to use. They are short and simple, which means that children learn them unconsciously and effortlessly while playing with their voices to become aware of and practise English sounds. By getting children to add gestures to rhymes, you can aid the memorisation process and give children a sense of achievement as they learn a rhyme to share with others in English. Here is a list of 10 rhymes that you can use in your classroom. Rhymes 1–6 are traditional nursery rhymes, rhymes 7 and 8 are action rhymes, and the last two will help you with classroom management. You'll find the words in the Appendix (p169), and you can learn the tunes by searching for these classic songs on YouTube.

1. Twinkle, Twinkle, Little Star

This traditional nursery rhyme has five verses. Choose the number of verses that you want your class to learn according to their level of English.

2. Humpty Dumpty

This traditional rhyme can be used to introduce an Easter-egg-making activity. The children can say the rhyme as they decorate their Easter eggs.

3. Baa Baa Black Sheep

This is a great rhyme to teach children while they are working on the topic of animals.

4. Jack and Jill

This traditional rhyme can be taught in conjunction with lessons about being helpful and obedient (doing chores) and being careful (avoiding accidents and what to do if they happen).

5. Hickory Dickory Dock

This traditional rhyme is a fun way to teach or revise the time. The original rhyme has 12 verses which you can teach your class depending on their language level.

6. One, Two, Buckle My Shoe

One, Two, Buckle My Shoe is an action rhyme which is great for teaching to children who are learning numbers. When the children say the rhyme, they show the numbers with their fingers and simulate the actions: One, two, buckle my shoe (pretend to buckle their shoes); three, four, open the door (pretend to open the door); five, six, pick up sticks (pretend to pick up sticks); seven, eight, lay them straight (pretend to lay them straight); nine, ten, a big fat hen (pretend to be a big hen).

7. Bouncing ball rhyme

In a bouncing ball rhyme, children bounce a ball and try to do the action they are saying as they say the rhyme.

Number one, touch your tongue

Number two, touch your shoe

Number three, touch your knee

Unit 25

Number four, touch the floor

Number five, learn to jive

Number six, pick up sticks

Number seven, go to heaven

Number eight, over the gate

Number nine, touch your spine

Number ten, do it again.

8. Skipping rope rhymes

Children love to play with skipping ropes. Getting them to say the following rhyme is a great way for you to practise numbers with your class. If you don't have lots of space in your classroom, take the children outside to learn this rhyme:

Bread and butter, sugar and spice,

How many children think I'm nice?

At this point the class counts the number of jumps that the child is able to jump.

9. Jumping Jack

This action rhyme can be used as a classroom management strategy to give children's energy levels a boost. The children stand up and act out the rhyme as they say it.

Jumping Jack, jumping Jack,

Clap your hands, clap, clap, clap.

10. Counting rhymes

Choosing a child to come up to the front of the class and volunteer can be tricky and even unfair in the eyes of some children. To avoid this situation, you can use a counting rhyme. Say the following rhyme and point to the children as you say the stressed syllables.

Apples, peaches, pears and plums,

Tell me when your birthday comes!

When you have finished saying the rhyme, the child who you pointed to on the last syllable answers the question by telling you which month their birthday is in. The children sitting either side of that child then say the names of the months in order, beginning with the month that child's birthday is in. The child who says 'December' is the chosen one for your next activity.

Stories and drama

Stories and drama are activities which naturally appeal to children's characteristics and imaginations. This section will look at how we can exploit these activities in the young learner English language classroom so that learning English becomes a creative and memorable classroom experience.

There are also practical activities that can be applied to any story and several classic and engaging story suggestions to teach common topics on most young learner language courses.

The final unit provides suggestions for popular drama activities that can be used to develop children's language, creativity and teamwork skills in any classroom.

10 reasons to use stories and drama in the young learner classroom

Stories and drama are activities which naturally complement each other, as drama provides children with the opportunity to react to a story in a multi-sensory way. This is motivating and appealing for them. In order to get optimal results in your classroom, choose stories and drama activities that you like, and that match the age and language level of your learners.

1. Language in context

Stories and drama activities use a holistic approach to language learning. They encourage children to pick up chunks of language that are at or just above their language level. The language is always presented in a clear and meaningful context rather than as a list of words to memorise. The result is that they tend to remember them long after the lesson has ended.

2. Understanding the world

Through the characters in a story or a short roleplay activity, children are encouraged to develop an understanding of the world around them that is connected to their own life experiences. Thus, stories and drama activities are an excellent way of introducing and dealing with sensitive topics and issues in the classroom.

3. Imagination

Listening to stories and participating in drama activities transports children to different and magical worlds without their ever having to leave the classroom. Thus, these activities appeal to a child's innate love of fantasy and play, which are valuable tools when it comes to developing their creativity.

4. Social and thinking skills

Social and thinking skills are sometimes referred to as the 4Cs: communication, collaboration, critical thinking and creativity. These skills are naturally developed in stories and drama activities. The activities also help children to develop basic thinking skills such as hypothesising, guessing and inferring meaning. Children are encouraged to work with, take turns with, relate to and respect others.

5. Memorable learning experiences

Stories and drama activities help develop interpersonal skills. They also encourage children to repeat the activity various times, developing memory and concentration in the process.

6. A springboard for learning

This type of activity is very flexible and a great springboard for learning, enabling you to use them to complement the topics and activities in your coursebook. Alternatively, you can organise learning in such a way that it derives from a central story or drama activity. Or you can bring them into your classroom every now and again, say, once a month or even just twice a term. Another advantage to using this type of activity is that you can follow it up with many varied activities. See Units 28 and 30 for some suggestions.

7. Speaking and listening skills

Both stories and drama activities provide students with a multi-skilled approach to learning. While listening to a story or drama activity, children develop active listening skills. By participating in one of these activities, they take a step further and develop their speaking skills, too. It's not all that surprising that they remember these experiences long after they have ended and beg to do them again in class.

8. Awareness of other cultures

Stories in particular are a fantastic way of bringing a multicultural element into your classroom. They help make children more aware of and tolerant towards other cultures by helping them understand and respect cultural difference through the main characters in the story.

9. Sense of achievement

When children participate in a story or drama activity, they get to practise and apply the language they are learning or have learned in a natural and fun context. They are also given the opportunity to use it independently, which in itself is a motivating experience. The climax of this process is when they get to perform their drama activity, retelling the story they heard in a creative way, to a real audience, showing everyone how good they are at speaking English.

10. Magical and fun

Perhaps the most important reason of all to use stories and drama activities in your classroom is the fact that stories and drama are fun. Everyone, regardless of their age or interests, loves a good story. Letting go and participating in a drama activity is an equally motivating experience.

'If a child is reluctant to read or has a little confidence to talk in the class, help the child by reading them a story, stopping where necessary to interact and ask questions.'

Raziye Uzun Yandim, Turkey

Unit 26

10 tips for making storytelling a memorable classroom experience

A good storyteller can transform storytelling into a truly magical experience by bringing the story to life in our minds and hearts. Begin by deciding whether you want to tell the children a story without the book or whether you are going to read it to them. Both options will require some preparation. Here are a few tips to help you find the true storyteller in you.

1. Choose the story wisely

The success of your storytelling adventure begins with the story that you choose to tell. Make sure that the story you choose ticks the 'good story' criteria by asking yourself a few basic questions:

▶ Does it appeal to the children's tastes and interests?

▶ Is the story related to the children's personal experience? Will they be able to identify with it?

▶ Is the language level within or just above the children's language level?

▶ Does the story have enough repetitive language structures that the children can learn?

▶ Does the story transmit positive values to the children?

▶ How do I feel about telling this story?

2. Prepare, prepare and prepare again

The secret to success in storytelling is the amount of time that you put into the preparation. Make sure that you know the story and that you are comfortable reading or telling it long before you go into the classroom. Use a visual storytelling plan (see Appendix, p172) or graphic organiser to help you visualise the story and remember it so that there are no hiccups when you tell it or read it to the children.

3. Adapt the story for the children you are telling it to

Remember to adapt the story to the audience in front of you. Change and add any details that you know will appeal to your students' personalities and interests. They haven't read the story before and won't know what you have changed, but they will remember how the story you told them made them feel.

4. Get children into a story mood before telling the story

Remember that a good story is more than just a mere activity. It is a complete classroom experience. This means that you need to get the children into a storytelling frame of mind. There are various techniques that you can try to do this: you could bring a story puppet to help you tell the story, or you could put on a funny story hat or coat just for storytime.

5. Have a different class arrangement for story time

Think about where the children will be when you tell them the story. A good option is to organise the class in a circle for circle time. Remember to stand up and go round the circle with the book so that all the children can see the illustrations. For larger classes, organise the front of the classroom in a semicircle, amphitheatre style: some children sit on the floor in the first two rows, then there are one or two rows of children sitting on chairs, and finally there is a row of tables which the tallest children sit on.

Unit 27

6. Pre-teach important vocabulary

Make sure that the children can follow the essential vocabulary in the story. Children need to know about 90% of the words in a story to understand it. This may require you to pre-teach any difficult vocabulary which you cannot explain through gestures.

7. Use gestures and body language when telling the story

Make sure that you keep the children engaged. Once you know the story, remember to take time to plan the gestures and body language you'll use and the pauses you'll make while telling it. Remember that you will only be ready to tell the story when all this comes naturally to you.

8. Use different voices for different characters

As a storyteller, your voice is your greatest ally. Remember to plan how you will use your voice. Think about pitch and volume, and the pace at which you speak. How will you express emotion in the story? Can you use different voices for all the various characters?

9. Stand in different parts of the room

To help make the story more visually engaging for the children, try using the space in the classroom to your advantage. Choose an area of the classroom for each main character and stand in each character's area when they speak in the story. This will help learners follow the plot.

10. Involve the learners as you tell the story

Involve the children in the actual storytelling process by stopping and asking them questions. Remember to give them time to think before you give them the answers. Another secret is to give the children actions to do while they are listening to the story: negotiate specific gestures for them to make at certain moments. You can also get them to repeat pre-agreed sounds, words or language chunks. Once you have finished telling the story, make sure that you personalise it by asking the children whether they liked it or not and why. Finish off by sharing your personal enthusiasm for the story with the children.

10 story activities

Stories are a fantastic way of exposing children to, and getting them to learn, new language in context. The activities that you associate with a story will help engage the children during the storytelling process and make the story meaningful for them. Here are 10 activities that you can apply to any story. Activities 1–4 can be used as pre-storytelling activities, and activities 5–10 are best used afterwards.

1. Guess what's in my box

Give the children a reason to listen to the story by appealing to their curiosity. Put a few objects related to the story in a box. Wrap the box in colourful wrapping paper and take it into class. Let the children touch and shake the box without opening it to guess what's inside. After a few guesses, invite different children to open it, take out an object and show it to the class. To re-use the box, make sure that the lid can open without the children having to tear the wrapping paper. Alternatively, let a child tear the wrapping paper as if it were a present. As the child shows the class an object, teach and drill any vocabulary that they don't know. Then tell them that they'll be hearing a story about the objects in the box and ask them to clap their hands or click their fingers each time one of the objects in the box is mentioned in the story.

2. Play a flashcard game

An alternative, which requires less preparation time compared with the activity above, is to take flashcards of the main target vocabulary in the story and to play a flashcard game with them before telling them the story. For flashcard game ideas, see Units 35 and 36.

3. Discuss the front and back covers of the book

Encourage the children to examine the front and back covers of the book before you start reading the story. Tell them the title of the story and ask them to predict what the story will be about. Encourage the children to develop their observation skills by focusing on details with narrative significance in the illustrations. This is also an opportunity to teach them words like front cover, back cover, blurb, author, illustrator and award.

4. Discuss story images

An alternative way of getting the children to predict the plot of a story is to scan one or two central images in the book and to show them to the children on paper or in a digital format. (Remember to ensure you are complying with your country's copyright regulations and your school's photocopying policy.) Encourage the children to describe what's happening in each image and to predict how that image relates to the rest of the story. If you are teaching older young learners, you can extend the activity by sticking the images on the board and making word maps with any target vocabulary that you want the children to learn.

5. Doing comprehension exercises

After telling the children a story, always save time for an activity or two to check that they have understood it. For younger learners, check comprehension through simple speaking activities. You could try getting older children to order images or characters according to the story, or to match pictures of the characters in the story to pictures of their actions. Alternatively, you could simply retell the story making a few mistakes and invite the children to correct you each time they hear one.

6. Sing a song or chant about the story

Some stories are based on a popular song or chant that you can teach the children before or after telling them the story. For examples of this type of story, see Unit 29 point 10. If the story you have chosen doesn't have a corresponding song or chant, why not invent one with the children?

7. Do an arts and crafts activity related to the story

A popular post-storytelling activity is to devise an arts and crafts activity related to the story. A simple yet effective choice for any story is to get the children to make finger puppets of the main characters using empty toilet roll tubes. They can then use their puppets to retell the story to younger students in the school, or share it with their families at home.

8. Roleplay the story

If you want to try something more ambitious, invest in a cross-curricular activity and put on a short play of the story for the other classes in that year, or even the whole school.

9. Make a storybook

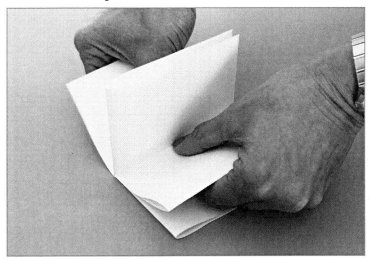

You can give children ownership of the story by challenging them to come up with an alternative ending to the story. Help children 'publish' their stories by making their own storybooks. (See https://www.myetpedia.com/etpedia-videos/ for a demonstration.)

10. Organise a story exhibition

Organise a story exhibition and invite children to contribute by producing artwork (pictures, paintings and sculptures) or projects relating to the story. Invite the school community to visit the exhibition and to vote for the best piece of artwork or project, which will win a prize. Remember to have participation certificates for every participant.

10 types of story for the young learner classroom

When choosing a storybook to read in class, remember to choose a variety of books so that every child in your classroom can experience a story which will foster their love for reading. Here are 10 suggestions for different story types to take to class.

1. Fairytales

Fairytales can work well in the classroom because children often know them in their own language as well. A few particularly popular children's fairytales are: *Goldilocks, Cinderella, Sleeping Beauty, Snow White and the Seven Dwarfs, The Gingerbread Man, The Ugly Duckling, The Country Mouse and the City Mouse* and *Jack and the Beanstalk*. For a more modern version of this fairytale, use *Jack and the Baked Beanstalk* by Colin Simpson (Templar, 2013).

2. Stories about values

The following stories deal with topical issues and values: *Lost and Found* by Oliver Jeffers (HarperCollins, 2015) – about friendship; *Susan Laughs* by Jeanne Willis (Andersen, 2011) – for making children aware of others who are different, and *This is Not My Hat* by Jon Klassen (Walker Books, 2014) – for broaching the topic of stealing.

3. Stories about animals

Storybooks about animals are usually successful with children. The following three animal stories have captured the hearts and imaginations of children around the world: *As Big as a Pig* by Allie Busby (Barron's Educational, 2001); *Gorilla* by Anthony Browne (Walker, 2013) and Eric Carle's lesser-known storybook *Polar Bear, Polar Bear, What Do You Hear?* (Puffin, 2007).

4. Stories about food

If you are planning to teach the topic of food, here are four storybooks that you might want to include in your unit plan. The first two are perfect for fussy eaters: *I Will Never Not Ever Eat a Tomato* by Lauren Child (Orchard, 2003) and *Peas! It's Not Easy Being Peas-y* by Andy Cullen and Simon Rickerty (Puffin, 2009). There's a surprise on each page in *Ketchup on your Cornflakes* by Nick Sharratt (Scholastic, 2006) and *Dragons Love Tacos* by Adam Rubin (Dial, 2015) is an unexpected treat!

5. Stories about school

Splat and the Cool School Trip by Rob Scotton (HarperTorch, 2013) is a storybook that invites the children to go on a school trip to the zoo. *I Am Too Absolutely Small For School* by Lauren Child (Orchard, 2015) and *David Goes to School* by David Shannon (Scholastic, 2001) help children understand why going to school and respecting school rules is important.

6. Stories from around the world

Take the children round the world without leaving your classroom by reading the children the following books: *I'd Like The Goo-Gen-Heim* by Alvin C Hollingsworth (Reilly & Lee, 1970); *The Queen's Hat* by Steve Antony (Hodder, 2014); *Handa's Surprise* by Eileen Browne (Scholastic/Walker, 2006); *The Sandwich Swap* by Queen Rania of Jordan Al Abdulah & Kelly DiPucchio (Hyperion, 2010); *Yoko* by Rosemary Wells (Hyperion, 2009) and *Bee-bim Bop* by Linda Sue Park (Houghton Mifflin, 2008).

7. Stories about festivals

Encourage children to become more tolerant and respectful of cultural diversity by reading them a story about a cultural festival. Here are a few stories that you can try out:

▶ Christmas: *A Wish to be a Christmas Tree* by Colleen Monroe (Sleeping Bear Press, 2005). This storybook has the added advantage of being in rhyme.

▶ Chinese New Year: *Lanterns and Firecrackers: A Chinese New Year Story (Festival Time!)* by Jonny Zucker & Jan Cohen (Frances Lincoln, 2014).

▶ Diwali: *Ria & Raj and The Gigantic Diwali Surprise* by Kiran Lyall & Venisha Sudra (BuzzWord UK, 2013).

▶ Ramadan: *Rashad's Ramadan and Eid-Al-Fitr* by Lisa Bullard (Cloverleaf, 2012).

8. Must-haves

No young learner classroom's storybook collection would be complete without the following stories that have delighted children all over the world time and again:

The Very Hungry Caterpillar by Eric Carle (Puffin, 1994); *The Gruffalo* by Julia Donaldson and Alex Scheffler (Macmillan, 1999); *The Enormous Turnip* by Kathy Parkinson (Albert Whitman & Co., 1987); *The Tiger who Came to Tea* by Judith Kerr (HarperCollins, 2006); *Rosie's Walk* by Pat Hutchins (Red Fox, 2009); *Don't Let the Pigeon Drive that Bus* by Mo Willems (Walker, 2004); *Brown Bear, Brown Bear, What Do You See?* by Eric Carle (Puffin, 1995); *My Cat Just Sleeps* by Joanne Partis (OUP, 2011); *Wolves* by Emily Gravett (Two Hoots, 2015) and *Hide & Seek* by Il Sung Na (Meadowside, 2011), which is a simple but fun counting book.

9. Rhyming stories

To add variety to your reading list, try reading the following books, written in rhyming verse: *There Was an Old Lady Who Swallowed a Fly* by Pam Adams (Child's Play, 2000); *Silly Sally* by Audrey Wood (Harcourt, 2007) and *The Animal Boogie* by Debbie Harter (Barefoot, 2011).

10. Children's song storybooks

Why not read the children a storybook based on a song that they have already learned in class? If the idea sounds appealing, try the following suggestions: *If You're Happy and You Know It* by Jan Ormerod & Lindsey Gardiner (OUP, 2003); *Bingo* by Rosemary Wells (Scholastic, 1999); *The Farmer in the Dell* by Alexandra Wallner (Holiday House, 1998); *I'm a Little Teapot* by Iza Trapani (Scholastic, 1997); *Itsy Bitsy Spider* by Iza Trapani (Charlesbridge, 2001); *Ms MacDonald Has a Class* by Jan Omerod (Red Fox, 1998); *On Top of Spaghetti* by Tom Glazer (Celebration, 1999); *Today is Monday* by Eric Carle (Puffin, 1996) and *The Wheels on the Bus* by Marsha Qualey (Picture Window, 2003).

Unit 29

10 favourite drama activities

Drama helps children to learn by doing, as they naturally associate words and language to the actions and movements they are experiencing. Drama activities can be as simple or as complex as you make them. A good way to go about it is to start small with short, simple activities, and to become gradually more ambitious as the children get used to acting and you get used to managing the class. Here are 10 simple drama activities to get you started. Activities 1–3 are mime and movement activities, activities 4–8 work on group dynamics, and the final two activities are drama-game activities.

1. Narrative mime

Divide the class into two: one group of actors and one group of readers. Spread the actors around the room. Choose a dialogue or story in your coursebook and invite the readers to read it out dramatically for the actors to act out in mime. Remember to demonstrate what you want both groups to do. Get the children to swap roles and repeat the activity.

2. Freeze

Children get very excited when doing drama activities, and this affects their behaviour. 'Freeze' is a great activity for helping you to maintain control of the class. First, you need a tambourine or a set of maracas. Give the children a simple scene to act out, such as: 'You're a little monkey in the jungle. You're climbing a tree. Oh! There's a banana. Stretch out and grab it. Peel it quickly and gobble it down!' As soon as you see that the children are becoming too excited, shake your tambourine or maracas to give them the cue to freeze. Only continue the activity when they have calmed down. Musical statues is a variation on this activity.

3. Charades

Charades is a drama activity that gets the children to practise vocabulary. Put a few picture cards or word cards that relate to the target language into a bag. Invite the children to choose one without looking at it or showing it to anyone. Get them to mime their secret word using gestures and facial expressions for the class to guess. The first child to guess it correctly continues the game.

4. Mirrors

This is a game played in pairs, which allows children to learn and practise talking about their daily routine. One child looks into the 'mirror' (represented by the other child) and mimes a daily activity like having a shower. The other child – the 'mirror' – mimes the exact action back, while saying what they are doing. Get the pairs to swap roles after a few minutes.

5. Imaginary places

Use background music to develop the children's imaginations. Get the children to sit in a circle. Dim the lights and play the music. Ask the children to close their eyes, listen to the music for a few seconds and imagine a place the music reminds them of, and think about what they are doing there. Wave your magic wand and bring one or two of the children to life. Ask them to move into the centre of the circle and act out their imaginations for the others to guess.

6. Give a voice to inanimate objects

Get the children thinking about what everyday objects might say if they could talk, with questions such as 'What would a dustbin say if it could talk?', 'What would the board say if it could talk?', 'What would your notebook/backpack/mobile phone say if it could talk?'. Get the children to write one or two sentences, practise them and act them out for the class. Invite the class to vote for the most original performances. Always remember to give encouraging feedback.

7. Dialogues

Write 5–8 target words or expressions that the class have been learning on the board. Divide the children into groups and get them to use them to prepare a short, simple dialogue that they can act out for the class. Remind them to use gestures and facial expressions. Remember to give them enough time to practise before inviting them to perform. An alternative is for them to make finger puppets (see page 85) and to use those to roleplay their dialogue.

8. 'Feeling' dialogues

Make a set of 'feeling' flashcards (showing an image that represents a feeling, for example, a happy smiley face for the word 'happy' – see Appendix, p174) and a set of mini 'feeling' cards – one for each child. Stick the 'feeling' flashcards on the board and drill the new vocabulary (see Unit 36). Mime the feeling and invite the children to guess which feeling it is. When the children are ready, swap roles by inviting a child to come up to the front and mime a feeling for the class to guess. Next, invent a short dialogue and drill it with the children. Distribute a mini 'feeling' card to each child and tell them to keep their feeling a secret. Invite the children to go round the class and say the dialogue you just drilled with the emotion on their mini 'feeling' card for other children to guess.

9. Zip, Zap, Zop

This is a great game for introducing a drama activity and developing concentration skills. The children stand in a circle and start clapping to a regular rhythm. One child points to another and says 'Zip'. That child points to another and says 'Zap'. The third child points to another and says 'Zop'. If a child makes a mistake or hesitates, then he or she is out. The game continues until there is only one child left.

10. Catch and clap

This is a classic drama activity, played in a circle with a ball. Choose a lexical topic with the class. The children stand in a circle and one child throws a ball to another child. When the ball is in the air, the child who threw the ball claps and says a word belonging to the lexical set. If the child can't remember a word, he or she is out. The game continues with the child who caught the ball throwing it to another child and repeating the procedure until there is only one child left. To make the activity more challenging, increase the speed of the game.

Unit 30

Arts, crafts and games

Arts, crafts and games are a fantastic way of developing children's fine motor skills, and for teaching children grammar and vocabulary without their realising it.

This section will start by giving you 10 good reasons to take activities like these into your classroom. Following that, you will find plenty of concrete ideas for arts and crafts activities and games. All of these can be used to teach the most common topics on a young learner course and to develop the children's language skills in a communicative and engaging context.

10 reasons to use arts and crafts activities

Arts and crafts activities can be a real asset in any young learner classroom. However, to be truly successful, these activities require careful planning and effective classroom management strategies. Remember that an arts and crafts activity has three fundamental stages: before, during and after the activity. All of these stages depend on specific instructions that you'll need to prepare beforehand. You'll also need to include a tidying-up stage to help the children develop responsibility skills and get the classroom back in order without too much fuss. For an example of a tidy-up chant, see Unit 23, point 3. Below are 10 tried-and-tested reasons to bring arts and crafts into the young learner classroom.

1. Memorable

Exposure to art, music and drama promotes increased brain activity. The more active the brain is, the more memorable a learning experience tends to be. You may find that children remember and speak about an arts and crafts activity that they did long ago as if it were yesterday.

2. Variety

Arts and crafts is another tool in your teacher toolkit that you can use to add variety to your teaching. Most children will love the opportunity to create an object while learning language and applying it to a concrete and meaningful context.

3. Effective for language learning

Remember that making an arts and crafts activity is a process. This means that when they are doing the activity, the children will naturally be exposed to language, inevitably picking up the words and expressions needed to make the object. This means that you can expose children to a lot of language in context throughout the whole process, and not just during the final presentation stage of the activity.

4. A welcome break

Arts and crafts are a great way to give children a change of pace from working with the coursebook and a more formal approach to learning. This type of activity allows children to learn without realising that they are working hard. It also allows them to work according to their own rhythm and pace, which naturally 'opens their learning gates' and raises motivation levels.

5. A behaviour management technique

An arts and crafts activity is a great classroom management and behaviour tool that you can use for calming children down after a more boisterous activity. Children will need to focus on what they are making. The class will tend to be calmer and easier to manage for a good 10 minutes!

6. A wide range of skills

Arts and crafts activities help children to develop and acquire a wide range of skills, as they learn to focus and work hard to create a final product. They learn to overcome various unexpected obstacles by applying problem-solving skills and being creative and adaptable – all essential skills in the information age. Not all children are artistic by nature: a child can excel at languages and maths, but have difficulties when it comes to drawing, cutting and creating things, depending on their natural talents and fine motor skills. Thus, children will need to communicate and work with others. As a teacher, your job is to ensure that they have enough language to do so in English.

7. Fine motor skills

While colouring in within the lines or cutting along the lines may be simple for some children, others, who may not have been to pre-school or developed their fine motor skills, will need lots of practice in the young learner classroom. An engaging way of giving them this practice is by challenging them with arts and crafts activities.

8. A way to experiment

Arts and crafts activities allow children to experiment and make mistakes, which can end up producing surprising and pleasing results. Thus, in the arts and crafts classroom, mistakes are not necessarily seen as a negative but rather as an opportunity to explore something else or even start from scratch and try again. These are skills that will benefit the child's language-learning process later on.

9. Fun

It is undeniable that arts and crafts make life, and lessons in general, more exciting and interesting. Children prefer to do a fun arts and crafts activity than a language drilling activity any day.

10. A sense of achievement

Arts and crafts challenge children to make something which they can then take back home to their loved ones. This is a perfect way for teachers to build children's self-esteem, self-discipline, co-operation and self-motivation.

Unit 31

'Most kids love crafts. Not only do they learn English but they also develop their motor skills and imagination, which are important for further development.'

Alexandra Aldongarova, Kazakhstan

10 popular arts and crafts activities

Unit 32

Arts and crafts activities are a great way to bring diversity into the primary classroom. However, not every arts and crafts activity is adequate for the young learner classroom. Before you choose an activity, make sure that it meets the following criteria: is it suited to your learners' age, gender, interests and skills? Does it respect time constraints, or is it too time consuming? And finally, does the activity allow the children to pick up language in context and practise it, or is it limited to developing the children's artistic skills? Here is a list of 10 arts and crafts activities that respect these criteria.

1. Decorated name card

Start the year by doing an arts and crafts activity and getting to know your students better. Have them decorate a name card (see also Unit 6), making it unique to them. Information given on the back, or illustrated through the design, will help you find out more about each child and their skills and talents.

2. Bookmark

Good readers make good students. It's important to introduce a reading culture in the young learner classroom, so why not start by getting the children excited about the actual reading process? Children can make a personal reading bookmark or page marker that they can put in every book they read. (See https://www.myetpedia.com/etpedia-videos/ for a 'how to make' demonstration.)

3. Storybooks

A fun and personalised arts and crafts project that you can do in class for any topic or storybook that you have read is to challenge the children to make their personal wordbook or storybook. Children can make a topic book or dictionary by writing and illustrating a word on that topic on each page. (See https://www.myetpedia. com/etpedia-videos/ for a 'how to make' demonstration.)

4. Origami fortune-teller

Children have made origami fortune-tellers for decades. Why not introduce this classic 'toy' into the classroom to get children to have fun while revising numbers, colours, the alphabet and target language. See the Appendix, page 176, for how to play a game with the fortune-teller, as well as ideas for questions to include in it. (See https://www.myetpedia.com/etpedia-videos/ for a 'how to make' demonstration.)

5. Paper plate masks

Encourage children to participate in drama activities by getting them to make their own props. Paper plate masks are easy and fun to make, and help shyer children to feel less exposed in front of the class. You can make whole-face or half-face masks, and even Venetian-style masks – by gluing the mask onto a lolly stick.

6. Puppets (finger puppets, paper bag puppets, lolly stick puppets)

Puppets are a great tool for encouraging children to try and speak English in class. Like masks, they give children a crutch to lean on, but they also allow children to speak without being worried about the mistakes they are making. They are also very teacher friendly as they allow you to correct the mistakes without criticising the child: 'Oh dear, Mr Penguin must be very tired today. Mr Penguin, did you forget that we say *I am hungry* and not *I are hungry*? You need some rest and a big bear hug!' By giving children this type of feedback, you are correcting the character represented by the mask and not the child behind it. See the Appendix for instructions on how to make some simple finger puppets (p177).

ETpedia: Young Learners © Pavilion Publishing and Media Ltd and its licensors 2016.

Unit 32

7. Musical instruments, noise-makers, shakers

Show the children how to make a musical instrument or a noise-maker that they can use when singing the songs in the coursebook or saying any chant that you invent with them. All you need is a toilet roll tube or a small plastic container with a lid and some dry beans. Seal the bottom of the toilet roll tube and put a handful of dried beans in it. Then seal the top and cover it with shiny paper or blank paper for the children to decorate as they wish. A time-saving alternative is to simply decorate it with some coloured duct tape.

8. Drawings and murals

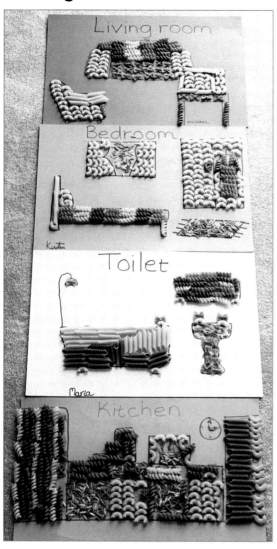

Get the children to make individual drawings or tile paintings, which you can then put together to create a class mural on a specific topic or story that you have been working on. The classroom will look a lot more attractive and the children will be reminded of the topic that you worked on each time they look at the wall. To make a more sophisticated 3D mural, try using dry pasta, bottle caps or plastic bottle lids.

9. Sculptures

Develop children's fine motor skills by having them make clay sculptures of items representing topic vocabulary that they are learning. Not only is this material cheap, but it also lasts for a long time.

10. Story dice

A fun way of getting children to retell a story you have told them is to ask them to make story dice of that story with an image of a particular part of the story or the name of a character in the story on each face (see Appendix, p178, for a dice template). The children roll their dice and see which scene or character from the story is uppermost. They then retell that particular part of the story or explain what happened to the character. Children have fun retelling the story and get to train their speaking skills without realising that they are repeating the same language over and over again. They also get great satisfaction from the fact that they are able to tell a story they heard in English.

10 topic-related arts and crafts activities

If you are looking for arts and crafts activities which can be applied to the main topics that are taught in the English young learner classroom, take a look at these 10 topic-related arts and crafts activities. They can be used in every primary classroom to teach a variety of topics.

1. Weather wheel

A good routine to start your lesson every day is to talk about the weather. To scaffold this language for children, make a weather wheel with them (see Appendix, p180). For more advanced learners, you can add two outer circles: one for the days of the week and the other for the months of the year.

2. Weather mobile

Make a weather mobile, which you can hang up in class so that the children are exposed to weather-related language every day. Use cardboard to make the mobile longer lasting. Get the children to draw pictures of the weather and to label the back of each picture. Laminate the children's drawings if necessary. You can make a vocabulary mobile for any topic that you teach.

3. Clock

To encourage children to practise asking and telling the time, get them to make a clock (see Appendix, p183). Use the clock to do a pairwork activity in which the children take turns setting the clock and asking each other the time.

4. Topic spinners

Spinners are a very popular resource to have in any young learner classroom. They can be used to practise vocabulary, or as an alternative to dice when playing games. Like mobiles, they can be made for any topic (see Appendix, p184). As the children get older, divide the spinner into more sections so that the children can practise more vocabulary. Get the children to draw a picture of a different word for the topic you have chosen in each section. Once the children have made the spinner, ask them to play a game by spinning the spinner and naming the image the spinner has landed on.

5. Themed hats

Let the children have fun with the words they are learning by helping them to make themed hats. These can be about one word they have learned (eg rabbit), or they might prefer to make wearable 'banners' of their favourite words relating to a topic. Use the banners/hats to play a pair game. The children put on their hats and choose a favourite secret word related to their banner/hat (eg 'carrot'). Their partner has to ask them questions to guess which word they are thinking of (for example, 'Is your word something that rabbits eat?'). Keep the hats and use them as props in drama and roleplay activities.

6. Topic-related mini-flashcards

Get the children to make mini vocabulary flashcards (see Appendix, p185), which they can use to play a fun bingo game. The children place mini word cards face-up on a bingo card. Slowly, say the words out loud. When a child hears a word that they have on their bingo card, they turn that word card face-down. As soon as a child manages to form a vertical or horizontal line of turned-over cards, he or she shouts 'Bingo!' and takes over from the teacher as the 'bingo caller'. Younger learners who cannot write yet can make mini picture flashcards; older learners can make word cards or even illustrated word cards.

7. Topic wheel

Topic wheels are a good way of getting children to practise vocabulary you have worked on for any topic. Divide the wheel in half and ask the children to draw pictures of the words you want them to practise on one side and the corresponding words on the other (see Appendix, p187). The objective is for the children to spin the wheel and match each picture to the corresponding word.

Unit 33

8. Word banners

Help the children revise vocabulary they have been working on by making a topic word banner (see Appendix, p189). Hand out a template to each child. Ask them to choose a word for any particular topic and write the word and decorate the banner with a picture relating to that word. Then put all the children's banners together and make a class banner. You can get the children to repeat the words on the banner by making a banner chant for the children to repeat to a set rhythm.

9. Crazy sentence-maker

To help the children learn to make sentences in English, get them to make a crazy sentence-maker (see Appendix, p190). Give the children three different coloured strips of cardboard on which they write parts of a sentence: on the first strip they write 8–10 subjects, on the second strip, 8–10 verbs, and on the last strip, 8–10 adverbs. Then let them play with their sentence-maker to create crazy sentences which they can repeat or write in their notebooks.

10. Word-wall poster

Get the children to make visual word walls about the topics they have been working on in class. Give each child a blank piece of paper or cardboard. Begin by brainstorming the words that children can remember about the topic they have been learning. Allocate one word to each child so that words are not repeated. Get each child to write and illustrate their allocated word on the blank paper and put it up on the wall chart to help children remember how to spell words correctly.

10 reasons to play games in class

If you've ever played a game with children, you'll know that they are a fantastic way to engage children in the learning process. Here are 10 more good reasons to play games in class.

1. Play

Young learners are naturally drawn to play. As toddlers and very young learners, children learn through play, both at home and at nursery school. Games allow children to experience play-learning again in the classroom. So, it is not surprising that children become more engaged when you announce that they are going to play a game in class.

2. Competition

Another good reason to introduce games in the classroom is that they appeal to children's characteristics. Children tend to be competitive by nature, and games have the power of encouraging children to speak English and work hard just so that they can win the game.

3. A natural context

Games are usually built around a context. As children are curious and imaginative by nature, they are easily drawn into this context. This means that games provide you with a natural context for children to practise and apply language that they have learned in class.

4. Drilling practice

Many games require the children to repeat a language structure or vocabulary again and again in order to play the game. This provides the children with lots of drilling practice. The children often don't even notice that they are doing this as they are so focused on the game itself. Another reason why games are useful for drilling language is that children really enjoy playing them, so they tend to ask you if they can play the same game several times or in another lesson.

5. Memory skills

Games are a great tool for developing children's memory skills, as children often have to play a game several times before they actually manage to win it. This means that games help children learn and remember new language. Pair-matching games are an ideal tool for training children's memories, as they force the child to remember where the card pairs are. Memory skills will later prove to be fundamental when the child reaches more advanced levels of the language.

6. A revision exercise

A great way to begin a lesson is to play a game that you played last lesson. Alternatively, play a game that gets them using the content that you looked at in the previous lesson in order to help children quickly revise what they learned.

7. Play at home

Another reason to invest valuable learning time in making and playing games in class is that children can then take them home to play with their families. This means that games allow children to take home the language they are learning in the classroom. They will often bring it back again as they give us feedback on what happened, who won, and what their families thought of the game.

8. Co-operation

Many games are built on the concept of co-operation. This means that no matter how good an individual student may be, they need to learn how to work with other team members in order to define a group strategy and win the game. Co-operation and teamwork skills will be an essential skill when children enter the workforce, and games allow us to train this skill from an early age.

9. Social skills

One of our main tasks as teachers is to teach the whole learner and not just the language learner. Games are an excellent tool for us to do this as they help us develop the children's social skills such as turn-taking. In addition, games help children realise that we all have different talents, which are essential to being the best and winning the game: a child may not be very good at English, but if they have a talent for drawing, they will be a valuable asset to the team when it comes to playing a game like Pictionary.

10. Fun and engaging

Perhaps the most important reason to play games in class is that they are fun and engaging by nature. As teachers, we should always remind children of how much fun learning is. Games are the perfect tool to do this as they allow us to prove to them just how enjoyable the learning process can be.

'I love teaching young learners. The classes are always a highlight of my week as the students are fun, eager and above all still respect you as a teacher! Songs, jokes, games, crafts ... where else will you be paid to act like a kid?!'

Glenn Standish, Poland

10 vocabulary and grammar flashcard games

Games appeal to children's competitive nature and give them a good reason to try hard at using language. Here is a list of 10 games that can be applied to almost any topic. Activities 1–5 are targeted at vocabulary and activities 6–10 are targeted at grammar.

1. Alphabet game

Make a set of alphabet letter flashcards so that you have one for each child. Hand out the letter cards randomly. Play some music and encourage the children to dance and move around the room to the music. When the music stops, ask them to line up in alphabetical order as quickly as they can. Remember to alternate cards so that the children practise the whole alphabet.

2. Back to the board game

This activity is suitable for more advanced classes. Divide the class into two teams and choose one child from each team to stand in front of the class with their back to the board. Put a (different) flashcard on the board for each team. A member of each team rolls a dice. The team with the highest number starts. That team gives their player one clue to help them guess the word on their flashcard on the board. If the child guesses correctly, the team gets a point and the next child takes their place with a new flashcard until all the team members have had a go. If the child doesn't guess correctly, the other team takes a turn to give their own team member a clue. The group to guess the most words wins.

3. Basketball game

Divide the children into teams. Choose one child from each team to come to the front of the class. Place the waste paper bin against a wall and get the children to line up in front of it. Show the first group a flashcard. They consult and give their answer (ie identify the word from the picture on the flashcard). If they are right, their representative at the front of the class is allowed to have a shot at the basket with a paper/soft ball and win a point. Then it is the turn of the second group, and so on. The group with the highest score at the end wins.

4. Catch

The children sit in a circle. Introduce or review a set of vocabulary flashcards by placing them in a pile in the centre of the circle. Ask a child to go to the centre, take the first card from the pile and show it to everyone. The child goes back outside the circle and walks round it touching each child's head while randomly saying words from the vocabulary set. When the child says the 'magic' word, ie the word on the flashcard, the child whose head was touched must stand up and chase the first child round the circle, trying to catch him or her. If the first child gets back to the vacant space and sits down without being caught, the 'chaser' chooses the next flashcard and continues the game.

5. Adverb action miming game

This game is great for revising vocabulary that the children have already learned. Begin by choosing a topic that you want to work on, such as daily routines, and write an action on the board, such as 'brush your hair'. Then invite a child to choose an adverb flashcard from an opaque bag. The child then mimes the action according to the adverb word card and the other children try to guess the adverb.

ETpedia: Young Learners © Pavilion Publishing and Media Ltd and its licensors 2016.

6. Simon says

'Simon says' is the perfect game for practising the imperative and reviewing vocabulary relating to the body. Ask the children to stand up, and then give them an instruction, for example, 'Simon says touch your head'. The children who do not carry out each instruction correctly sit down. After a while, speed up your instructions and add a twist to catch children out, simply saying, 'Touch your foot!' (instead of preceding the instruction with 'Simon says'). Any child who carries out the instruction without 'Simon says' is out. When the children are ready, swap places with one of them who then becomes the caller. The last child left standing is the winner.

7. Musical chairs

Place 8–10 chairs in a circle in the centre of the room, each with a flashcard related to the language topic you have been working on eg 'food'. Choose some children to sit on them. Invite the remaining children to sit in a circle on the floor around that circle. Play some music and ask the children to walk around the chairs and to sit down on one when the music stops. Remove a chair and stop the music. One child will be left standing. The children who are sitting must say a sentence about their flashcard; for example, if it's a picture of an orange, they might say, 'I like oranges' or 'Oranges are delicious'. If the child is unable to produce a correct sentence about their flashcard, they are out, and the child who was left standing has a go. If the sentence is correct, he or she is allowed to sit again. Choose a new player from those sitting on the floor to join the game, and replace the players every now and again.

8. Matching game

Choose ten sentences and divide them into two. Make a sentence card for each part. Jumble all the parts together. Get the children to order the parts to make 10 sentences. This game can be played individually or in groups. Use flashcards to play it as a whole class.

9. Jumbled sentence cards

Choose a sentence and make a single-word flashcard for each word. Put all the flashcards in an opaque bag and jumble them up. Hand out the cards randomly to the children and invite the children with flashcards to come up to the front of the class and show everyone their flashcard. Challenge the children to form a sentence in 10 seconds. To involve the rest of the class, allow the students sitting down to give the players tips.

10. Jump to the left and jump to the right!

Get the children to stand up. Say a sentence. The children jump to the left if the sentence is correct and jump to the right if the sentence is incorrect. Children who jump the wrong way have to sit down. The last child left standing is the winner.

10 flashcard games

As a teacher of young learners, you may already know the value of flashcards. Flashcards help you teach new vocabulary by providing the children with a picture of the new vocabulary item so that children can quickly understand their meaning. They also allow you to do a multitude of activities while catering to young learners' needs. Here are 10 flashcard activities to get you using this versatile resource.

1. Voice-drilling activity

Children need to practise a word many times before they can remember it properly. However, this drilling process can become tedious. So why not add some interest by using the children's imaginations and voices? Challenge the children to repeat the target vocabulary using a different voice each time. All-time favourites are: a witch's voice, a princess's voice, a dragon's voice, a ghost's voice and a parrot's voice. (In the latter case, the children repeat the each word at least twice in a squawky parrot tone.)

2. Guessing game

Remember that children need to be exposed to vocabulary before they can produce it themselves. A fun way of giving them this exposure is to play a guessing game. Present and drill the target vocabulary that you want the children to learn. Then practise it by playing a guessing game with them. Start by choosing a flashcard without looking at it. Show it to the children by holding it in front of you. Ask the children simple questions like 'Is it [adjective]?' and 'Is it a [noun]?' until you can guess which flashcard you have chosen. When the children are ready, encourage them to take your place.

3. Missing card

After you have presented, put up and drilled a set of flashcards on the board, test the children's aquisition of this vocabulary by removing one flashcard at a time and leaving an empty space. Begin with the first flashcard and continue removing them in order until there are no flashcards left on the board. The objective is for the children to try and remember the order of the words represented by the flashcards. To make the activity more cognitively challenging, remove the flashcards in a random order, rather than in the order that you presented and drilled them.

4. Memory game

A variation on the activity described above is to play a memory game as you present and drill a set of words. After drilling the words two or three times, turn the cards over, one at a time, until the children can see only the back of the flashcards. To make the activity less cognitively challenging, turn the flashcards over in the order they are on the board.

5. Show quickly and hide

After you have presented and drilled your target vocabulary, choose a flashcard of one of the words, without the children seeing it, and hide it behind your back. Then quickly move it to your left or right so that the children can catch a quick glimpse of it. Then hide it behind your back again and ask the children to name the flashcard.

6. Reveal a tiny bit

A variation of the activity above is to hide a flashcard by placing another flashcard turned over in front of it. Then, in slow motion, reveal a tiny detail or area of your flashcard, and ask the children to guess which flashcard it is. Continue revealing a small amount at a time until the children are able to correctly guess which flashcard it is and repeat the word.

7. Point to

After you have shown the children a flashcard and started drilling it, display it in a place where the children can easily see it in the room. Introduce all the target flashcards and display them round the room. Then play a 'point to' game by saying, for example, 'Point to the apple. Yes, that's right – the apple! Point to the apple.' To make the activity even more fun, associate another action to the pointing activity, for example, 'Stand on one leg and point to the …'; 'Touch your toes and point to the …'.

8. Flashcard hide-and-seek

Start by presenting and drilling your target vocabulary. Then, choose three helpers and three players. Ask the players to leave the room for a few seconds. Next, ask your helpers to hide the flashcards around the room. Invite the players back in and challenge them to find the flashcards. Involve the rest of the class by allowing them to guide the players, saying, 'Hot!' (if the players are standing near the flashcard), 'Boiling!' (if they are really close to finding it), 'Cold!' (if they are standing far away from the flashcard) and 'Freezing!' (if they are heading in the opposite direction).

9. Go fish

Organise the children in a circle. Place the flashcards that you have drilled in the centre face up so that everyone can see them. Choose a player. Ask that child to go to the centre and 'fish' (ie fetch) a particular flashcard. If the child chooses the correct flashcard, they get to choose the next player. This game can also be played as a group game.

10. Fly swatter game

Begin by presenting and drilling a vocabulary set. Then display the relevant cards on the board or on a wall in the classroom. Divide the children into two teams and choose a player from each team to stand at a set distance from the flashcards. Choose one representative for each group and give each one a plastic fly swatter. Say one word at a time. The quickest player to swat the corresponding flashcard earns a point. The winning team is the team with the highest score. To make the game even more challenging, speed up the rhythm at which you say the words. If you can't get hold of fly swatters, get the children to swat the flashcards with their hands.

Activities for topics

Many young learners courses nowadays are designed around several central topics or themes. As the children work through these topics, they learn new vocabulary and grammar structures, which they are encouraged to use in context.

This section aims to give you ideas for activities that you can use to introduce and teach these topics. Note that you can easily apply an idea presented in one topic to any other topic. This will give you a broad repertoire of activities to take into your classroom.

The final two units in the section are aimed at developing the children's awareness of the world and their cultural understanding, so that they can become more competent citizens and learners.

10 activities for the topic of FOOD

Food is a favourite topic on any young learner course. It's a subject that naturally interests and appeals to children, while relating to their everyday lives. Here are 10 activities that you can try out in your classroom to help children to learn and consolidate this topic area.

1. My pizza

Invite your young learners to become creative Italian chefs and make their own paper-plate pizzas. Use a white paper plate for the base of the pizza. Ask the children to bring supermarket pamphlets and magazines into class, so that they can cut out their favourite toppings for their pizzas and stick them on their paper plates. Ask older young learners to label their toppings. Then use the paper-plate pizzas to roleplay ordering a pizza in class.

2. Fruit sculptures

Develop the children's fine motor and artistic skills by getting them to make clay sculptures of their favourite fruit. Then organise a food sculpture exhibition for the school community. Create a ballot box for visitors to vote for the top three sculptures for each year group. Remember to have participation certificates for all the participants.

3. Food menu

Another fun activity involves children making their own healthy meal or snack. Typically, this activity will work well with children aged 9 to 11, who can begin by researching how much fat each food item contains and make a bar chart with their findings. Use the graphs to discuss the following questions with the children: How many grammes of fat does each item contain? Which item contains the most/least fat? Which item is the healthiest? Why? Finally, challenge the children to sculpt their meal or snack.

4. Hungry monster worksheet

A nice activity to complement the activity above is to ask children to make a 'hungry monster' worksheet of a healthy meal or snack. The children have to choose the healthy snacks, cut them out and 'feed' them to their hungry monster by sticking them on its tummy. See the Appendix for a hungry monster template and some pictures of healthy snacks (p192).

5. Food Venn diagram

Graphic organisers are a great way to get children to organise and structure the words they are learning. Use a Venn diagram to challenge children to compare and contrast delicious food and healthy food. This is a great way of helping children realise that delicious food can also be healthy.

Delicious food
Chocolate
Ice cream
Cakes

Strawberries
Smoothie
Grilled food

Healthy food
Vegetables
Salads
Soups

Follow up the activity with a 'healthy food hunt' around the school grounds. End the day with a healthy food picnic.

6. Rainbow of healthy food

This activity allows you to associate the topic of food with colours. Ask the children to bring old magazines to class (ones produced by supermarkets are good for this activity). Give the children a blank template of a rainbow to colour in (see Appendix, p193). Then, in their magazines and pamphlets, they find a food item for each colour, cut it out and stick it on their rainbow. Older learners can practise their writing skills by labelling their cut-outs.

7. Food calendar

To make children aware of their eating habits, ask them to make a food calendar of the food they eat for breakfast, lunch, dinner and snacks that week. Younger learners can simply draw the food they have eaten, while older learners can write words and illustrate them. Use the children's calendars to start an informal discussion to raise awareness of healthy eating habits. Repeat the activity a few weeks later to compare and contrast the children's eating habits and discuss any changes.

8. Slam

Choose 8–10 words to teach. Drill them with the children using flashcards. (For more ideas on how to use flashcards, see Units 35 and 36.) The children sit in a circle and put their hands on their heads. Place the flashcards in the centre of the circle and choose three children. Then say one of the words. The children race to fetch the corresponding flashcard. The first child to touch it and say the word correctly gets to keep the card. In large classes, play the game in groups or divide the class in two by forming two concentric circles.

9. Food pairs game

Use the mini-flashcard template (see Unit 33, Point 6) in an arts and crafts activity to get the children to make food dominoes. The children draw a food item in the mini flashcard frame and write the word on the flashcard next to it. Put the children in pairs or small groups. Get them to put their flashcards and word cards together, shuffle them and play a food memory game: first, spread the cards on the table face down. The first child turns a card over, has a quick look and tries to form a picture/word card pair by guessing (or remembering, later in the game) where the corresponding card is. If they don't form a correct pair, the child turns the cards back over and the other child has a go.

Unit 37

10. Setting a table

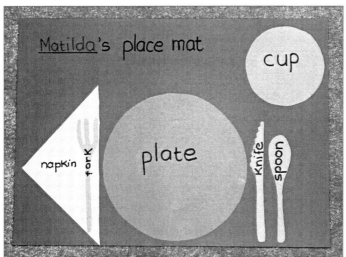

Not all young learners will know how to set a table. Use this topic to teach them how to set and sit at the table. Depending on their age, introduce vocabulary related to the cutlery and crockery they usually use (knife, fork, dessert spoon, soup spoon, plate, cup, napkin), and then challenge them to make a placemat poster. Bring in realia to roleplay good table manners and let the children play.

'Check allergies at the start of the year and you'll be free to include food related crafts in your classes. From decorating biscuits to making chocolate truffles, these tasty crafts are always a hit. You could also try exploring your senses together using different foods and spices. What do they look/smell/taste like?'

Shona Lacy, Young Learners Co-ordinator, Poland

10 activities for the topic of ANIMALS AND PETS

Animals and pets is a common topic on most young learner English language courses. Children are naturally drawn to this topic as many have pets of their own and love animals. Here are 10 suggestions to help you make the most of the attraction that children have for this topic in your classroom.

1. Animal paper-plate masks

Get the children to make an animal puppet that they can then use to roleplay short animal dialogues or to present their favourite animal in a show-and-tell activity. Masks will help you encourage shy students to participate in these speaking activities. All you need is a white paper plate, some elastic, cardboard and crayons or markers to decorate the paper plate.

2. Japanese koi fish

Koi fish are a common symbol in both Japanese and Chinese culture. They are also the official symbol for Children's Day (5 May) in Japan. Develop children's intercultural awareness by sharing the koi fish legend with them and inviting them to make a koi fish to present in a show-and-tell activity. Then decorate the school on Children's Day (see Appendix, p195).

Unit 38

3. Non-fiction book

Develop children's writing skills and encourage them to practise the '[Animal (plural)] can + [verb (infinitive)]' structure by inviting the children to make a non-fiction book about their favourite animal. (See https://www.myetpedia.com/etpedia-videos/ for a demonstration.)

Teach the children how to make the front and back cover. They then write and illustrate a short sentence about what their animal can do on each page. Older learners can make more complex sentences by writing one thing that their animal can and can't do; for example, 'Lions can roar but they can't sing'.

4. Crazy animal strip book

Make a crazy animal strip book with the children to help them visualise and describe what animals would look like if various parts of their body were made up from different creatures. Photocopy 5–10 copies of the template provided in the Appendix (p195) for each child and get them to draw and colour a different animal on each sheet. In the first square they should draw the animal's head. In the second square they draw the animal's arms and body, and in the final square they draw the animal's legs, feet and tail. Then put the children in pairs and get them to create crazy animals by mixing the strips in their books and describing them to each other; for example, 'This is my crazy *elelionebra*. It's got an elephant's head, a lion's body and a zebra's legs and tail. Isn't it crazy?'

5. Pop-up animal poem book

Develop children's poetic skills by getting them to make a pop-up book to illustrate a short poem about an animal. Children can write their poem by filling in a simple poem frame individually or as a class. Here is an example:

I am a [frog].

I eat [flies].

I can [jump up high].

(See https://www.myetpedia.com/etpedia-videos/ for a 'how to make' demonstration.)

6. Animal graphic organiser

Give each child a blank sheet of paper for them to draw and colour in their favourite animal. Ask them to write a sentence about their animal, for example, 'My cat is a pet/wild animal/farm animal'. Then, create a giant Venn diagram (see Unit 41, Point 4) for the various categories of animals the children have drawn. Finally, get the children to put up their pictures in the correct category.

7. Animal zoo/farm

Create word cards of the target vocabulary that you want to practise, and distribute one to each child. Give each child a blank piece of paper for them to draw the animal on their word card. Analyse the characteristics of the various animals with the children and discuss how they fit into the food chain. Then draw a big farm or zoo on at least two sheets of cardboard and ask the children to organise the animals on the farm or zoo in such a way that they don't eat each other.

8. Animal snap game

Give the children blank copies of the flashcard template (see Unit 33, Point 6). With the children, make a list of ten animals on the board. Ask them to write their name on the back of each blank flashcard, and then to draw one of the 10 animals on the front of each card and colour it in. They then make the corresponding word cards. Put the children in pairs. Ask them to mix up their cards, turn them over and shuffle them without looking at them. The children then divide the cards equally and play a game of snap. The children take turns turning over a card and identifying it. If both cards show the same animal or word, the first child to say 'SNAP!' and correctly identify the animal wins the pair of cards. The winner is the child with the most cards.

9. Animal peg

Use this simple arts and crafts activity to make a classroom management tool to help you check who is in class every day. Children decorate a wooden peg by drawing their favourite animal on it, colouring it in and writing their name on it. As soon as the children arrive in class every day, they take their peg and attach it to a class attendance board so you can see who is in class. You can also use the pegs to give them permission to go to the toilet.

10. Watch a trailer

Show the children an official Disney trailer like the one for *Zootopia* and get them to count how many animals they see. Then use the trailer as a context for teaching the children the new vocabulary they need to identify the animals in the trailer.

'Click like a dolphin and cluck like a chicken but also use images and movement as animal noises differ greatly around the world.'

Jennie Wright, teacher and author, Germany

10 activities for the topic of TOYS

It is no surprise that children love the topic of toys. Here are 10 activities relating to this fun and engaging area.

1. Odd flashcard out

This first activity is a flashcard activity that will help develop the children's thinking skills. It can be played in pairs or small groups in a competition format. All you need is a set of toy flashcards (see Appendix, p198). Organise the flashcards so that there is an odd flashcard in each set. To start with, the odd flashcard can be unrelated to toys, but as the children get used to the game, challenge them to look for deeper connections between the toys; for example, you could categorise the flashcards into toys that bounce, toys that break, toys that make a noise or toys that move. To make the activity even more challenging, introduce a time factor: the first group to correctly identify the odd flashcard and provide a valid justification is the winner.

2. Over and under

This is another flashcard game. Divide the children into two groups and get them to stand in two lines, one child behind the other. Give each group a toy-related flashcard or word card, which the first child in each line passes back over their head to the child behind them. That child then passes it between their legs to the child behind them, who in turn passes it over their head, and so on, until the last child gets the flashcard. The last child then has to make a sentence using that word in order to show that he or she understands its meaning. If the child is able to do this, the group gets a point. The group with the highest score is the winner. Don't take points off for grammatically incorrect sentences. Jot the children's mistakes down and work on them in the next lesson.

3. Toy bingo

Bingo is a popular, fun game which gets children playing while learning or consolidating new vocabulary. Photocopy a bingo card for each child and get the children to make a set of mini toy flashcards (see the Appendix, p199, for a mini-flashcard template). Alternatively, use the ready-made toy flashcards (p198). Older learners can use word cards instead of picture flashcards. Ask the children to place their flashcards face-up on the bingo card in any order they like. Then call out a word at a time. If a child has that flashcard, they turn it over so it is face-down. The first child to form a vertical, horizontal or diagonal line of turned-over flashcards is the winner. To raise activity levels, ask the children to stand up when they have two flashcards turned over in a row.

4. Toy jigsaw

Photocopy the jigsaw template on p201 for each child, and challenge them to make a toy-themed picture/word jigsaw for their classmates to do. On one puzzle piece, the children draw a toy of their choice. On the piece that connects to it, they write the corresponding word. In total, each child makes 16 jigsaw pieces for 8 different words. After the children have made and coloured in their puzzles, stick them on a sheet of stiff cardboard and get them to carefully cut out each piece. Finally, ask the children to make and decorate an envelope for their puzzles. Use the puzzles to keep fast finishers busy. Alternatively, you can use the ready-made toy jigsaw on p200.

5. 'Spot the difference' worksheet

'Spot the difference' worksheets help children pay attention to detail and simultaneously develop their language skills. Younger learners can simply circle and identify the differences, while older learners can be challenged to write sentences about the differences in each picture. See the Appendix for a toy-related worksheet (p202).

6. Counting worksheet

Relate new toy vocabulary to numbers by getting the children to count the number of toys they can see in an image (see Appendix, p204). Older learners can be asked to write short sentences about each toy to practise their writing skills.

7. Colour by numbers

A colour-by-numbers worksheet (see Appendix, p205) will help children revise the colours while learning new vocabulary.

8. Recycled toy robot

Raise the children's environmental awareness and develop their creativity by challenging them to make a recycled robot with old used boxes and items which they bring to class. This activity can be done individually or in groups and followed up with a toy exhibition.

Unit 39

9. My favourite toy 'animoto'

Get the children to develop their computing skills by making a 30-second video about their favourite toy. 'Animoto' is a free software application which allows you to choose a template, add images and sound and write a short sentence about each image. The children's animotos can be projected onto a wall or a screen in the toy exhibition mentioned in Activity 8.

10. Celebrate Japanese 'Hinamatursi' day

Raise the children's intercultural awareness and celebrate this Japanese festival (which translates as 'Toy Doll Day') on 3 March. You can follow the activity up with an arts and crafts activity that gets the children making paper dolls from around the world. (See the Appendix, p206, for templates. Alternatively, use the internet to find templates that best appeal to the interests of your students.)

10 activities for the topic of THE BODY

Most young learner and very young learner courses have at least one unit on the topic of the body. Not only is this topic great for a mixed-ability classroom, but it is also perfect for helping children to recognise and follow instructions. After teaching the parts of the body, you can complement this topic by teaching the children about clothes. Here are 10 activities to help you bring this topic to life.

1. Life-size poster

Challenge the children to help you make a life-size poster of the body for your classroom. This will help to decorate the classroom while exposing the children to new vocabulary, which they can then revise every day. Get a large roll of paper and cut a sheet large enough for one of your students to lie on. Ask that child to spread their arms and legs out in a star shape and to lie still. The other children trace the contours of that child's body. Next, the children draw some shorts and a t-shirt on it and colour in and decorate the sheet. Finally, get the children to make a word card for each part of the body that you want to teach, and to label the poster with them. Use the poster to play games, for example, a 'point to' game or a fun fly-swatting game (see Unit 36, Point 10).

2. 'Simon says' game

Help the children master instructions and learn the parts of the body by playing 'Simon says'. Start by giving an instruction, for example, 'Simon says touch your head'. Then see which children are really paying attention by giving an instruction without saying 'Simon says', for example, 'Touch your toes'. If the children follow this type of instruction, they are out, and have to sit down and watch the others. After a while, involve the children who are out by letting them give the instructions. The winner is the last child left standing.

3. Body wheel

Use the wheel template (see Unit 33, Point 7) to help the children make a body wheel to learn the target vocabulary that you want to teach them. The children move the wheel so that they can see a picture and the corresponding word in the magic windows. After a while, the children can cover the word window, say the word and then check and see if they already know the word.

4. Crossword puzzle

A nice homework activity or an activity for fast finishers is to get the children to make a crossword puzzle for other students. Children begin by making the crossword puzzle using 8 to 10 words. Younger learners can then simply write the words below the grid for their classmates to fit into it. Older children can write gapped-sentence clues to help their classmates remember the words in context and then use them to complete the crossword.

5. Listen and draw

Children love monsters. Monsters provide a fun context for children to practise the parts of the body. Put the children into pairs and hand out a monster worksheet to one of the pair and a blank sheet of paper to the other (see Appendix, p208). Ask the child with the worksheet to read their descriptions to their partner, who has to draw the monster being described. Then get them to compare the drawing with the original.

6. Monster drama activity

Bring drama into the classroom and practise vocabulary related to the body. Divide the children into groups. Explain that they have to work together and use their bodies to follow your instructions and create a monster sculpture: make a monster with three heads, five legs and four arms. The group that makes the first accurate body sculpture wins a point. The group with the highest score is the winner of the activity. To make the activity more challenging, invite the winners to swap roles with you and to describe the next monster that their classmates have to create.

7. Monster-drawing game

Divide the children into groups and give each group a monster kit for them to create their group monster (see Appendix, p210). They then describe their monster for the other groups to draw on the board. The first group to draw an accurate monster wins a point. The winner is the group with the highest number of points.

8. 'Who's who?' game

Give the children speaking practice by getting them to play a 'Who's who?' game in pairs. Each child takes a turn to choose and describe a character (see Appendix, p214) for their partner to identify. Adapt the activity for the mixed-ability classroom by giving less advanced students character cards with sentence descriptions to read out (see Appendix, p215). When the children are ready, take away the description cards.

9. Play jump

Spread the flashcards of the words you want to practise on the floor. Choose two players and get them to stand at a set distance from the flashcards. Say a word and ask the children to jump to that flashcard. The first child to get there gives the next instruction and continues playing the game. Replace the second child with another child so that all the children can have a go.

10. Body code worksheet

Give the children a secret code worksheet (see Appendix, p216) for them to crack the code and discover some words about the body. You can also add a secret message on the board using the same code for fast finishers to work out.

Unit 40

10 activities for the topic of CLOTHES

Items of clothing are a regular topic in most coursebooks. Here are 10 simple activities to help you teach this topic and bring some fun into the classroom.

Unit 41

1. Paper dolls

A fun arts and crafts activity to do with children is making paper dolls and various items of clothing that they can dress them with (see Appendix, p217). Remember to have two models – a girl and a boy – that the children can choose from. Develop children's listening skills by transforming this into a pairwork activity: one child tells the other child how to dress the doll and the other follows the instructions. Once the doll has been dressed correctly, the children swap roles.

2. Pelmanism (matching game)

Help the children learn new words by inviting them to play a Pelmanism (or matching) game. Give the children a set of 10–20 blank cards depending on how many words you want them to learn. To practise 10 words, ask the children to draw 10 items of clothing and colour them in on 10 separate cards, and then to make the 10 corresponding word cards. Alternatively, use the ready-made cards in the Appendix (p219). Get the children to place them face down on their desks and to turn them over one at a time and then back over again. The object of the game is for the children to find the 10 picture cards and match them with their corresponding word cards.

3. Word search

Get children to make a word search for their partner or the class to solve. The children choose 10 words related to clothes and write them on the lines below the word search. They then write the words in the word search. Ask them to write their name at the top and invite the class to solve each other's word searches. Alternatively, use the ready-made word search on p222 as a quick filler.

4. Seasons and clothes

Invite the children to organise the words they are learning using a graphic organiser such as a Venn diagram (see p109). This will help them to associate clothing with various contexts, such as the seasons. By using a graphic organiser, you will be encouraging the children to think more about the meaning of words rather than simply memorise them. With younger learners, start by simply comparing two categories; add more categories or circles to the Venn diagram for older children.

5. Clothes line

Introduce or revise 8–10 items of clothing with the children. Once the children know the words by heart, do the following activity: put a clothes line up across the classroom. Hang some pegs on the line. You can either bring a bag of old clothes into class or you could get the children to draw and colour in various items of clothing. Put all the clothes or the children's drawings together and do a listening activity: choose a child and tell them which clothes you want them to hang on the line; for example, 'Hang up a pair of trousers, a dress, a shirt and two socks.' Transform this activity into a competition by putting up two washing lines and dividing the class into two groups. Make sure that you have two equal sets of clothing so that both groups have a fair chance of winning the game.

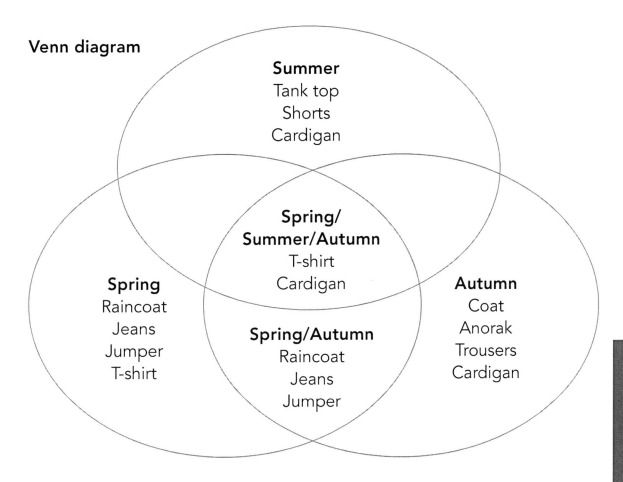

Venn diagram

Summer
Tank top
Shorts
Cardigan

Spring/ Summer/Autumn
T-shirt
Cardigan

Spring
Raincoat
Jeans
Jumper
T-shirt

Autumn
Coat
Anorak
Trousers
Cardigan

Spring/Autumn
Raincoat
Jeans
Jumper

6. Find someone who ...

Choose five children and ask them to go round the classroom following your instructions, for example, 'Find someone who is wearing a jumper!' The children go round the room and touch someone who is wearing that particular item of clothing. The fastest child calls out the next instruction.

7. I spy with my little eye

Play 'I spy with my little eye' with the children to practise their speaking skills. Introduce and drill the opening sentence, 'I spy with my little eye someone wearing a ...'. Then demonstrate the game to the children by choosing a child and describing what they are wearing by saying, 'I spy with my little eye someone wearing blue trousers and a red jumper.' The children have to look round the room and find the child that matches the description. The first child who guesses correctly continues the game.

8. Clothes fun

Divide the class into 2–3 teams. On the board, write the team names and members. Write words for 4–6 items of clothing below each group. Each team chooses which member of their group they are going to dress. Next, empty a bag of old clothes on the floor and when everyone is ready, shout 'Go!' The first group to correctly dress their group member in the items of clothing listed on the board is the winner. Make sure you have enough clothes in the bag for each group to be able to play the game successfully.

9. Tell a story

There are plenty of clothes-related stories you can tell children. *Froggy Gets Dressed* by Jonathan London (Puffin, 2007) is a great story about a little frog who wants to go out and play in the snow. It gets children practising the following items of clothing: socks, boots, hat, scarf, mittens, pants, coat and underwear.

10. Sing a song

Why not teach the children a song about clothes? There are lots of songs online that you can use. Here are some suggestions to get you started:

▶ *Put on Your Shoes* (http://supersimplelearning.com/songs/original-series/one/put-on-your-shoes)

▶ *Don't Put Your Trousers on Your Head* (http://learnenglishkids.britishcouncil.org/en/songs/dont-put-your-trousers-your-head)

▶ *New Pair of Shoes* (http://www.songsforteaching.com/charactereducationsongs/newpairofshoes.php)

'I've found that children love organising and putting on a fashion show. Encouraging them to put together unusual outfits and not to worry about being gender-specific in their choices makes this a fun and creative activity.'

Penny Hands, Scotland

Unit 41

10 activities for the topic of THE FAMILY

Families are an important part of children's lives, so it is natural that we should deal with this topic in the classroom. However, keep in mind that this topic can easily lead to stereotypes of the typical family which may not correspond to our children's reality. Here are 10 activities to help you teach this topic in context.

1. Family tree

A visual way to teach family vocabulary is to use the idea of a family tree in the shape of a 3D representation of an actual tree (see Appendix, p226). It will help you teach words like *aunt* and *uncle*, which can be difficult to explain. Ask the children to display their father's side of the family on one side of the tree and to use the other side for their mother's family members.

2. Listening activity

This activity can be used as a follow-up to Activity 1 above. Once the children are able to recognise the main family terms, give them a blank copy of a family tree diagram (see Appendix, p226). Below it, provide images of the family members with their names. Then read out the text in the Appendix. The children listen, and when they think they have identified a family member, they draw a line from the picture to the correct part of the family tree diagram.

3. Circle ball-game

To help the children practise saying and remember new vocabulary, get them to stand in a circle. Hold a soft ball and say a word (eg *mum*). Then pass the ball to the child on your right, who has to repeat the word you said and say another word. (eg *mum, dad*). Most children will be able to remember a sequence of about five words, so start a new word chain after about 5–8 children. To make the activity less challenging, allow the children to repeat words. After a few rounds, throw the ball to a child at random. That child has to say a word and pass the ball to another classmate. Make a bet with the children to see how many words they can say without breaking the chain.

4. 'Go fish' game

Use the mini-flashcards template (see Appendix, p185) for the children to make mini-flashcards of the family vocabulary that they are learning. They make one card for each family member and label them with 'mother', 'father', 'cousin', etc. Older learners can make simple word cards instead without any pictures. Then put the children in pairs or small groups and get them to mix their cards together so that they have a larger set of cards. Next, shuffle the cards and distribute two cards to each player. Put the remaining cards in a deck the middle of the table. The youngest player begins the game by taking a card from the deck. The aim is for the players to make as many matching sets of the same family member cards as they can. A 'set' is made up of as many cards as there are players: so, if there are four players, a set is made up of four cards. The first player draws a card from the deck in the middle and asks the other players if they have a matching card; for example, 'Do you have a *mother* card?' If nobody does, then that player has to 'go fish' (draw another card from the deck in the middle) and repeat the process. The player who gets the most sets wins the game.

ETpedia: Young Learners © Pavilion Publishing and Media Ltd and its licensors 2016.

Unit 42

5. Family mobile

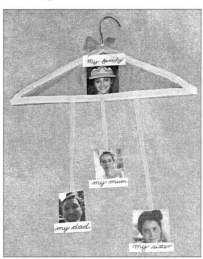

Children use a metal coat hanger, some ribbon and photos of their family members to make a family mobile. This is a great activity for show and tell, and can be used as a Mother's Day or Father's Day present too.

6. My family poster/portrait

A less challenging arts and crafts activity involves children making a poster of their family. Another option is to get them to bring a family picture and make a decorative cardboard frame for it. Develop the children's speaking skills by encouraging them to present their creations in a show-and-tell session. Older learners can write a short description of their families in their notebooks.

7. Family finger rhyme

Why not use this topic to teach the children a traditional finger rhyme? The children hold up a different finger as they say the rhyme, starting with their thumb.

Here is the family in my household.

Some are young,

And some are old.

Some are tall,

Some are small,

Some are growing just like me.

Together we live as a family.

8. How many family members?

Use a family counting worksheet (see Appendix, p231) to help children learn to ask, 'How many family members are there?', while developing their numeracy skills. After they have answered each question, get the children to practise the family vocabulary by identifying the family members in each photo. They then draw and complete a section for their own family.

9. Family survey: who lives in your house?

This topic provides you with an opportunity to find out more about your children's family backgrounds. Get the children to conduct a survey to find out how many family members there are in each household and who the children live with. See Appendix, p152, for a survey template.

10. Family thesaurus

Older children can make and illustrate a 6–8-page mini-thesaurus with synonyms for talking about their family members.

(See https://www.myetpedia.com/etpedia-videos/ for a 'how to' demonstration.)

The book can be laid out as follows:

page 1: *front cover*

page 2: *mother: mum, mummy*

page 3: *father: dad, daddy*

page 4: *brother and sister*

page 5: *grandmother: grandma, granny; grandfather: grandpa, grandad*

page 6: *aunt and uncle*

page 7: *cousin(s)*

page 8: *back cover: author: [child's name].*

10 activities for the topic of THE HOUSE

The home is a topic which appears in every coursebook. Here are 10 activities to help you make this topic fun.

1. Vocabulary games with dice

Give the children a copy of the dice template each (see Unit 32, Point 10) and ask them to draw and colour in pictures of rooms on each face of the dice. They then construct the dice. In pairs, the children take turns to roll their dice. Their partner has to say and spell the word for the room the dice lands on. An alternative is to ask children to draw words about furniture.

2. House riddles

In this activity, children practise writing sentences with the vocabulary they have learned by creating short, house-themed riddles for the class to solve. Examples of riddles might be: 'You sleep here' (Answer: bedroom); 'You make food here' (Answer: kitchen); 'You have a bath here' (Answer: bathroom). Then divide the class into groups and play a riddle game. Each group says a riddle for the other groups to answer. The first group to answer correctly gets a point. The group with the highest score wins.

3. A 'houses around the world' poster

Encourage the children to become global citizens by finding out more about different houses around the world. They use the internet to search for images and descriptions. They then choose their favourite one and make a poster which they can present at show and tell. When the class has listened to all the presentations, they can vote for the most original house, the nicest house, the strangest house, etc.

4. Geometric shapes house

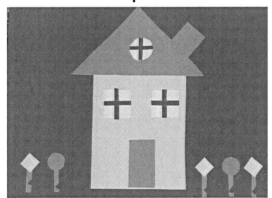

Give the children coloured paper and get them to cut out shapes to create a geometric house, which they can then use for a show-and-tell activity. An alternative activity is to put the children in pairs and give each child a geometric shape set. The children then create a 'shape' house without showing it to their partner. They take turns describing their house for their partner to make with their own set of shapes. The children then compare houses.

5. Decorate a room

Provide each child with copy of a 'room' worksheet (see Appendix, p233). Put children in pairs. Ask them to cut out the pictures and to stick them on to decorate their rooms. Then get them to write a few sentences about their rooms and to make a room poster to put up in class.

6. Listening and colouring-in

This activity gets the children to practise listening. Give them an outline image (see Appendix, p234), and then read out the accompanying script. The children listen, drawing linking lines from the objects to their correct place in the room and colouring in the picture according to your instructions.

7. 3D house models

Children make houses from the template (see Appendix, p235) and place them around an area in the classroom to create a town. They can then practise giving each other directions around the town.

8. House battleships

Battleships is a very popular game for children to play in pairs. It can easily be adapted for them to practise asking questions about houses. All you need is a copy of the 'House battleships' worksheet for each child (see Appendix, p236). Remember to introduce and drill the question modelled on the worksheet so that the children play the game in English and not in their first language. In this version of Battleships, the children hide some friends in their house, and the object of the game is for their partner to discover where the friends are by asking questions like 'Is Grace in the bedroom?' or 'Is Pat in the kitchen?'

9. Running dictation

A great way of getting children to progress from word level to sentence level is to do a running dictation. Make several copies of the 'My house' text (see Appendix, p237) to put around the classroom. Then put the children in pairs and get one child to be the runner and the other the scribe. The runner's job is to run to the place where the text is displayed to read and remember a chunk. He or she then runs back to the scribe and dictates it so that the scribe can reproduce the original text on a sheet of paper. Halfway through the activity, the children swap roles. When the time is up, get the pairs to swap texts with another pair. Dictate the original text to the class and have them correct each other's work. The pair that makes the fewest mistakes is the winner. To make the activity even more challenging, ask the children to include punctuation too.

10. 'My dream house' competition

Challenge the children to do a group project and presentation of their dream house. The children work in groups to create and present a dream house to the class. After all the presentations, hand out voting cards for each child to vote for the best house.

'I ask students to form groups to discuss their dream house, and each group should come up with a design. Later on, they have to give a description in front of the class and the class votes for the best house design.'

Solomon Au Yeung, Hong Kong

10 activities for the topic of SCHOOL

Unit 44

Children spend a lot of time at school and it plays a fundamental role in their lives, so it makes sense for them to learn how to speak about it in English. Here are 10 activities that you can take to class to help them do this.

1. Join the dots and guess the objects

A join-the-dots exercise (see Appendix, p238) is a fun activity to help children to learn new vocabulary. Once they have discovered the objects, they can label them or match them to the corresponding words. Fast finishers can keep busy by colouring in the worksheet.

2. Link-and-trace worksheet

This type of worksheet (see Appendix, p240) will help younger learners to begin to recognise the shapes of words and practise their writing skills. The children trace and colour in the words and then match them to the corresponding images.

3. Class survey

Divide the class into groups and get each group to choose a question for the class survey; for example, Group 1: What's your favourite subject? Group 2: What's the easiest subject? Group 3: What's the most difficult subject? Group 4: Where do you usually have lunch? Group 5: How do you usually get to school? Group 6: What's your favourite snack? When each group has thought of a question, they go round interviewing the other students in the class. They then make a bar graph showing the results of their survey. Finally, make a big survey poster where each group can publish their graphs.

4. Word scramble

Solving word scrambles is a great way to get children to work on their spelling. A good follow-up activity is to get the children to put the words in alphabetical order.

5. Hangman

Hangman is a fun way for the children to practise new vocabulary and work on their spelling, too. You can play this game in pairs or as a whole class. One child (the 'executioner') thinks of a secret word and draws a dash for each letter on the board. The rest of the class has to guess the letters that make up that word by asking questions, for example, 'Is there an 'e' in your word?' If they guess correctly, the executioner writes the letter on the corresponding line. If the letter is repeated in the word, he/she has to write it wherever it appears. If the class guesses incorrectly, the executioner starts drawing a simple stick figure, adding a part of the body for every wrong guess until the stick figure is 'dead'. The typical order is:

1st wrong guess: draw the post (an upside-down 'L').

2nd wrong guess: draw a small circle for the head below the horizontal line of the 'L'.

3rd wrong guess: draw a line down from the bottom of the head for the body.

4th wrong guess: draw one line out from the middle of the body for an arm.

5th wrong guess: draw another line for the other arm.

6th wrong guess: draw a diagonal line from the bottom of the body for the leg.

7th wrong guess: draw another diagonal line for the other leg.

8th wrong guess: connect the head to the post with a noose. This means that the man is dead and the players have lost the game.

The class can also take a chance and guess the word at any time, but if they guess wrongly, the executioner draws another part of the stick figure's body. The class wins if they can guess the word before the executioner finishes drawing.

6. Spelling bee

Spelling bees are a motivating way to encourage children to work on and improve their spelling. Give the children a list of 8–10 words to learn. The children practise writing the words at home. On the day, divide the children into groups and ask them to decide the order in which they will take their turns. Give each group a different word to spell from the list. The first child repeats the word aloud, spells it, and then says the word aloud again. If the child spells it correctly, their group earns a point. Then the next child in each group takes a turn. The group with the highest score is the winner.

7. Hot seats

This is a more challenging game that you can play with older learners. Put two chairs back to back in front of the class so that one is facing the board and the other the class. Give the child who is facing the class a flashcard of a school object. The student holds the flashcard so that the class can see it and, without saying the name of the object, describes it for the other student to draw on the board. If the describer gets stuck, the rest of the class can help. Put new students in the hot seats each time a new flashcard is introduced.

8. Circle memory game

Get the children to stand in a circle of 8–10 children. Challenge them to see if they can go round the circle without breaking it. The first child begins by saying 'Yesterday, I went to the shops and bought a ...', ending the sentence with a word for an object, such as 'book'. The next child then has to repeat that sentences and add another, for example, 'Yesterday, I went to the shops and bought a book and an apple.' The game continues with each child adding an item. If a child is not able to remember the sequence or say a new word, he or she is out. The last child remaining is the winner.

9. Drawing: What's in my backpack?

Children love to draw, so try personalising the topic by getting them to draw a picture of their backpack or school bag and what they usually put in it. To develop their writing skills, the children can make a list of the objects in their backpack. Older learners can write a few short sentences or a short text about their backpack.

10. School noughts and crosses

Divide the children into pairs and get each pair to make nine mini-flashcards of school objects. Next, give each pair a copy of the noughts-and-crosses card game (see Unit 17, Point 8) and follow the instructions to get the children practising their vocabulary while playing noughts and crosses.

10 activities for the topic of GLOBAL AWARENESS

Intercultural awareness is a skill which should be developed in our classrooms in order for children to become tolerant global citizens, able to respect and work with people from other cultures. Here are 10 activities that will help you introduce cultural awareness in your classroom.

1. Exhibitions

Exhibitions are a fantastic way to make the school community aware of cultural differences; for example, if the class is working on the topic of clothes or nationalities, the children can make traditional paper dolls (see Unit 41, Activity 1) and then organise a 'World Paper Dolls Exhibition'. If they are working on the topic of food, they could organise an international food fair, in which children bring in typical dishes from around the world for everyone to try. Get the children to make a simple fact card for their dish giving its name and place of origin.

2. World festivals

Celebrate different festivals from around the world. A great follow-up activity is to get children to make a multicultural book with a festival on each page, including a sentence, an illustration and the main symbol of that festival. Here's a list of 10 festivals you may want to celebrate:

▶ February: Chinese New Year (first day of the Chinese calendar), N'cwala (Zambian Harvest Festival)

▶ February/March (the Saturday before Ash Wednesday): Brazilian Carnival

▶ March 3: Hinamatursi Day (Japanese Doll Day)

▶ Early March: Holi (Indian Festival of Colour)

▶ May 5: Kodomo-hi (Japanese Boys' Kite Festival)

▶ First day of the month of Shawwal (signalling the end of Ramadan): Eid-al-Fitr (Muslim Festival)

▶ October/November: Diwali (Hindu Festival of Lights)

▶ November 1: Day of the Dead (South America)

▶ November–early January (25th day of Kislev): Hanukkah (Jewish Celebration).

3. Songs from around the world

Teach the children well-known songs from around the world: Morocco: *Rum Sum Sum*; Spain: *Mi Cuerpo*; France: *Alouette, Sur le pont d'Avignon*; Australia: *Kookaburra*; Malaysia: *Pok Amai, Amai*; Africa: *Toom, bah-ee-lero* (a call-and-response song: the children can develop their musical skills by playing the drums as they sing the song); Peru: *Yaw, Yaw Puka Paleracha* (a traditional native Inca song); Mexico: *La Cucaracha* (a silly song about a cockroach).

4. Stories from around the world

Read stories from around the world to the children, then get them to create and stamp their own story passport each time they read a story from a different country. For a few suggestions, see Unit 29, Activities 6 and 7.

5. International greetings bunting

Teach children about countries and nationalities by having them make bunting representing greetings from around the world. Give each child a template of an individual triangle to make their section (see Unit 33, Point 8). On one side, they draw a flag of a country they want to become an ambassador for. Next, they research how to say 'Hello' in the language (or one of the languages) of that country, and write the greeting on the back of their flag. Join the children's triangles along a length of string to make bunting. Decorate the classroom or school. Get each class to make a different banner (eg a 'Goodbye' banner, a 'Happy Birthday' banner, a 'Congratulations' banner, etc.) so that the whole school becomes more multiculturally aware.

6. Korean paper fan

A nice arts and crafts activity to help children working on the topic of colours is a Korean paper fan. All you need is a long sheet of paper which the children decorate and fold like an accordion.

7. Chinese animal signs

Explain to children that Chinese New Year is the most important Chinese festival and that it follows a lunar calendar, which means that it is on a different day each year in either January or February. The years are organised in cycles of 12, and each year within that cycle is represented by an animal. They always follow the same order: rat, ox, tiger, rabbit, dragon, snake, horse, sheep, monkey, rooster, dog and finally, pig. When the 12-year cycle ends, it starts again. Invite the children to make their personal Chinese New Year poster. The children write their name and the date of their birthday, and then draw the symbol of the year they were born in.

8. Cross-cultural animal posters

This is a great cross-cultural activity to do with the children when they are learning the topic of animals. Teach them some similes with the target vocabulary, for example, *as strong as an ox, as sly as a fox, as mischievous as a monkey*, etc. The children then compare and contrast these similes in English with their first language by finding a simile about the same adjective or animal. Finally, they make a poster of their favourite English and first-language simile.

9. (Coffee)-tin drums

Music and drums are an important part of life in many cultures. The children can make their own drums using recycled objects. They can play these while singing and dancing to a song like *Toom, bah-ee-lero*. All you need is an empty (coffee) tin with a plastic lid for the drum head and paint or colourful paper with which to decorate the actual drum.

10. Geometric Ghanaian Kente cloth strips

A paper version of a strip of traditional Kente African cloth, which is made from symbolic geometric shapes and colours, makes a wonderful arts and crafts activity for your cross-cultural classroom or for an international exhibition.

Unit 45

10 activities for the topic of ANGLO-AMERICAN CELEBRATIONS

Language and culture often go hand in hand, which means that the language classroom is the perfect place to make children aware of Anglo-American culture. Here are 10 Anglo-American celebrations and activities that you might want to try out.

1. Valentine's Day (14 February)

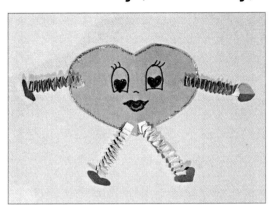

Teach the children various Valentine's Day messages, for example, *Be my love bug; Roses are red, Violets are blue, Sugar is sweet, and so are you!* and *Be my Valentine!* Then get them to make a Valentine's Day card with their special message in it and decorate it for a friend.

2. Shrove Tuesday (Pancake Day)

Shrove Tuesday, also known as Pancake Day, is the last Tuesday before Lent. In the UK, people make pancakes and have pancake races (in which participants race through the streets with frying pans, tossing pancakes). You can celebrate this day with children by holding a pancake race or by getting them to make the perfect pancake topping (see Appendix, p241). They can then present this during show-and-tell session.

3. St Patrick's Day (17 March)

Celebrate St Patrick's Day by getting the children to draw and colour in a picture related to St Patrick's Day. Once the children have finished their drawings, ask them to label them with words such as leprechaun, green, hat, pot, gold, coins, rainbow, etc. that relate to this festivity.

4. Easter (between 22 March and 25 April)

Celebrate Easter by organising an Easter egg hunt around the school by hiding chocolate eggs for the children to find.

5. Mother's Day (2nd Sunday in May)/Father's Day (3rd Sunday in June)

Celebrate Mother's Day and Father's Day with the children by getting them to make an acrostic poem to take home. All you need is a sheet of paper and some crayons or markers. The children start by writing MUM or DAD vertically on the paper. Then they think of an adjective that begins with each letter to describe their mum or dad. Finally, they decorate their poem and write a final message such as 'I love you' or 'You are the best mum/dad in the world!'

Here are some examples:

Marvellous	**D**ashing
Unique	**A**mazing
Magical	**D**evoted
I love you, Mum!	You are the best dad in the world!

6. Independence Day (4 July)

Start by reading the children a story about America's beginnings called *The Story of America's Birthday*, by Patricia A Pingry (Candy Cane Press, 2000). Then get the children to make their own '4 July' mini-book, and to write sentences which recycle verbs related to the senses; for example: 'On 4 July, it is the birthday of the USA. You can *see* lots of American flags. You can *watch* parades. You can *taste* apple pie. You can *hear* the fireworks.', etc.

(See https://www.myetpedia.com/etpedia-videos/ for a 'how to' demonstration.)

7. Halloween (31 October)

Halloween is a celebration which is quickly spreading across the world. Children in America dress up and go trick-or-treating round their neighbourhood. You can replicate this by organising a Halloween parade at school and choosing the most original costume.

8. Bonfire Night (5 November)

Bonfire Night commemorates the anniversary of an attempt by Guy Fawkes, in 1605, to blow up King James I and his government. It is celebrated with bonfires and fireworks. Get the children to make a representation of a simple bonfire using finger paints, and teach them this rhyme to mark the occasion:

Remember, remember the fifth of November,

Gunpowder, treason and plot,

We see no reason why gunpowder treason,

Should ever be forgot!

9. Thanksgiving (4th Thursday of November)

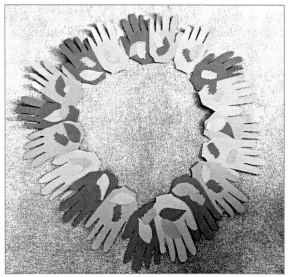

Discuss the spirit behind Thanksgiving and get learners to think about one or two things that they are thankful for. Then give them some white paper on which they trace their hand. On it, they write their name and the things they are grateful for. They then decorate it as they wish. Put all the hands together to make a class Thanksgiving wreath.

10. Christmas (25 December)

Celebrate Christmas by telling the children a Christmas story. Here are some tried-and-tested suggestions: *How Murray Saved Christmas* by Mike Reiss (Puffin, 2004); *The Polar Express* by Chris Van Allsburg (Andersen Press, 2015); *Snowmen at Christmas* by Carolyn Buehner (Dial Books, 2005), and for more advanced learners, *Auntie Claus* by Elise Primavera (Houghton Mifflin, 2011). Using an empty toilet roll tube, the children can then make a puppet of their favourite character in the story to decorate their Christmas tree.

Unit 46

Evaluation

Evaluation is an essential part of the language-learning process. This section aims to help you think about how to evaluate young learners while respecting their particular characteristics and needs, and maintaining their natural curiosity to learn English. The first unit will present you with 10 evaluation tips, which you can use to complement the evaluation procedures that are used in the school or institution where you are teaching.

The second unit is designed to help you provide the children and their families with detailed and useful feedback on their progress. This will help you boost their motivation and self-esteem and ensure that you keep all stakeholders informed.

10 evaluation tips for the young learner classroom

Evaluation is an important tool for providing feedback to a whole variety of stakeholders: school administrators, teachers, parents and families, local authorities and the children themselves. It helps us determine what has been learned, how effective learning has been and how we as teachers can best address our students' needs. Evaluation can be formative (done on an ongoing basis, to determine how well students are progressing) or summative (usually in the form of a formal test at the end of a year or a unit of work). Here are 10 evaluation techniques to help you obtain reliable information about the learning process.

1. Define clear learning objectives

Prepare the evaluation process by thinking carefully about what the children should master by the end of a particular topic that you are working on. For example, you might want them to be able to sing a song, act out a dialogue, have a short conversation in English, learn 10 new words, read and understand a short story and pronounce 10 words correctly. Next, choose the various tasks and activities that will help the children reach the learning objectives that you have set.

2. Create objective success criteria

When defining success criteria, think about the various learning stages that a child will have to go through before he or she will be able to successfully master those steps; then design your success criteria around these steps. Make sure that you focus on the various tasks that a child *can* manage rather than on what the child isn't able to do yet.

3. Observe the children in familiar learning contexts

Reduce the stress of evaluation by assessing the children in familiar teaching and learning contexts. Instead of setting aside a specific day for evaluation, assess the children as they do the various tasks you set in class.

4. Evaluate different interaction patterns

Remember that children have different individual ways of learning, but that they will need to develop teamwork skills to meet the demands of the workplace in the future. Thus, children should be evaluated in different interaction contexts such as when doing pairwork, when doing groupwork and when working individually.

5. Observe a few children every day

It is difficult to evaluate a whole class at once. Instead, focus on 3–5 different children in each lesson by observing them carefully and taking down detailed notes about their performance and progress. This will allow you to have detailed information about each child's progress by the end of the unit.

6. Use focused observation forms and checklists

Keep the evaluation process as objective as possible by creating objective evaluation forms for each unit you are teaching. Make sure that you focus on the children's progress by jotting down abbreviations like C (competent), N (non-competent) or W (working on) for each point. An alternative is to draw a forward slash (/) then a back slash (\) so that you make an X in each square, and finally colouring in the whole square so that you can use the same form throughout the unit you are working on. (See Appendix, p242, for a photocopiable focused observation form.)

7. Language portfolio

Language portfolios are an effective way of evaluating a child's progress over time. They involve getting the children to choose their best work (drawings, pieces of writing, examples of arts and crafts, examples of show and tell, small projects or even self-evaluation forms) to put in their portfolios. Remember that making portfolios is a time-consuming activity, so train the children to choose examples of their work, set time aside for giving feedback and reserve a space in the classroom for physically keeping the portfolios, as they can become very bulky as the year progresses.

8. Promote self-assessment

Introduce a culture of 'learning to learn' in your classroom by making self-assessment a regular part of learning. Remember that children will need to be trained to self-assess objectively, so invest time in teaching them what success looks like. Base self-assessment worksheets around 'can do' statements, for example, 'I can sing the Body Song'. Take time to think carefully about the language of your 'can do' statements. If they are in the learners' first language, children will easily be able to understand them. If they are in English, the language used will have to be simple and familiar for the children.

9. Evaluate linguistic and non-linguistic skills

Remember to evaluate the whole learner and not just the language learner. This means that you need to evaluate the four skills (reading, writing, listening and speaking) as well as things like social skills, thinking skills, teamwork skills and creativity.

10. Think carefully about summative written tests

Summative written tests are very stressful for young learners. Think carefully about how you will evaluate all the skills in this type of formal test and design your test so that you can assess what the children know, rather than trying to catch them out. Think of reading comprehension questions: some teachers might be tempted to take off marks if the child does not write the answer correctly, even if their answer is correct in terms of comprehension of the text. The Cambridge Young Learner tests are a good model to base your tests on, as they help you avoid delicate issues such as this one and test all four skills effectively.

Unit 47

10 ways to record children's progress and give feedback

Recording children's progress and giving stakeholders feedback can be a tiring and cumbersome task. Here are 10 practical suggestions to help you make this task less onerous and to ensure that you have detailed information to share.

1. Progress charts

A great way to get a general picture of a class's overall achievement is to create a class progress chart, which allows you to see how well the class is doing and who is falling behind or speeding ahead. This knowledge will enable you to create extra tasks and challenges for children who need to be challenged at different levels. It also helps you maintain motivation and ensure that everyone is ready for the formal test. See the Appendix, p243, for a sample classroom progress chart.

2. Class observation charts

Evaluation is a continuous process, which means that you need an easy and effective way of recording a child's progress in class every day. Classroom observation forms, which you can just tick, are a great tool for doing this. Create objectives forms to help you evaluate things like participation, homework, punctuality and behaviour. A useful trick is to record only the children who stand out for having done very well or very badly. You can use different colour pens or smiley faces to mark the difference. If the square next to a child's name is blank, then you automatically know that the child complied with the criteria being observed on a particular day. See the Appendix for a sample class observation chart (p242).

3. Behaviour charts

Behaviour is a key success factor in any classroom. Having a class behaviour chart and making it a class ritual to fill it out is fundamental to making children aware of how important behaviour is, and how it can influence their learning outcomes. Make sure you praise children who have made a conscious effort to improve their behaviour, even if they may not have managed to be perfect. In this way, you show the class that you notice and value the children's efforts. At the end of the week, take the time to analyse the class's behaviour for that week and to set behaviour objectives for the coming week. This procedure can also be done for weekly learning objectives. See the Appendix for a sample behaviour chart (p244).

4. Teacher journal

When you teach various classes every day, it is easy to confuse the things that happen in one class with what happens in the next. To avoid this, try keeping a small teacher journal. Reserve the last two minutes of your lesson for the children to pack up and clean the classroom. Use that time to write a quick note about anything or any child that stood out in class that day. This will allow you to have detailed and objective feedback to give to stakeholders about every lesson.

5. Individual interviews and meetings

A personal and effective way of giving feedback is to set aside a few minutes for student interviews while the class is doing groupwork. Always remember to start by stressing two good things the child has managed to achieve or improve. Then suggest one thing for the child to work on, and finally, end on something that you think the child is particularly good at and should continue doing.

6. Term report

The objective of a term or semester report is to give the child and the child's family information about the child's progress. The report should focus on giving information on both linguistic and non-linguistic skills. You can involve the child and the child's family by including a section where they can write their feedback (see Appendix, p243). For younger learners who can't read yet, try making picture reports with images instead of words.

7. Skills report

Skills reports help draw parents' attention to different skills that their children are working on. A time-saving alternative is to make a unit report which focuses on all the four skills (see Appendix, p247).

8. Child-centred reports

An alternative to formal reports aimed at stakeholders is child-centred reports, which show the children what they can already do in a light-hearted and visual way. A good example is a 'can do' garden with a flower for each thing that the child can do in the unit. An alternative is a language passport with a stamp for each different thing the child can do. Remember to focus on the whole learning experience when filling in these reports.

9. Digital contact

Many schools have digital systems in place to help parents follow their child's progress. If this is not the case at your school, try sending a simple general email to parents once every two weeks, informing them of what's going on in the classroom. Limit individual emails to urgent cases so that you aren't flooded with unnecessary work. To control the number of emails that you have to answer every day, tell parents when your email checking hours are each week so that they have a clear idea of your online availability right from the start.

10. Parents' open day

Parents' days are a fantastic way of inviting parents into the classroom to discuss and celebrate their children's learning. Remember to give feedback in such a way that parents can feel proud of their child's achievements, however small. This is also a great opportunity to involve parents in setting their children's learning and behaviour plans, and making them accountable for them.

'Building and maintaining communication with parents is an integral step for all teachers. It allows access to knowledge about the student, helps the parents keep up to date with their child's progress and address any concerns they might have, and, of course, encourages the child to share what is covered in class with their families.'

Pedrameh Badrian, Oman

Unit 48

Further reading

This section aims to help you find more ideas, information and references that can help you to continue developing professionally.

The first unit provides further reading suggestions that will help you find out more about young learners and various topics related to teaching this age group.

The second unit is aimed at providing you with online resources that can continue to broaden your teaching horizons.

10 more books about teaching young learners

If this book was your starting point to getting ideas to take into your young learner classroom, then you might be thinking about what to read next. Here are 10 suggestions filled with great ideas that have been read by teachers around the world.

Unit 49

1. *Teaching Young Language Learners* (2006) by Annamaria Pinter (Oxford University Press)

   This book is a comprehensive guide that combines research with classroom practice. It deals with a broad range of topics, such as children's learning and development, learning a first/second/third language at home and at school, primary ELT courses, teaching the four skills, learning to learn, materials evaluation and materials design.

2. *Children Learning English* (2005) by Jayne Moon (Macmillan)

   This is a handbook filled with lots of practical teaching suggestions for teaching children that will get you thinking about your children's needs and how to cater for them.

3. *Teaching Languages to Young Learners* (2001) by Lynne Cameron (Cambridge University Press)

   This book is about what happens in the classroom when children are learning a foreign language. It offers a theoretical framework to help you understand key issues relating to teaching young learners. It also gives advice on how to analyse and evaluate classroom activities, language use and language development, along with many practical examples taken directly from the classroom.

4. *Resource Books for Teachers* series (various publications), series editor: Alan Maley (Oxford University Press)

   This series covers a wide range of areas that will be of interest to teachers of young learners. It provides practical guidance as well as ideas, activities, resources and photocopiable materials that you can use in class. Titles in the series include: *Young Learners* by Sarah Philips, *Games for Children* by Gordon Lewis and Gunther Bedson, *Grammar for Young Learners* by Gordon Lewis and Hans Mol, *Creating Songs and Chants* by Carolyn Graham, *Assessing Young Learners* by Sophie Iannou-Georgiou and Pavlos Oavlou and *Arts and Crafts with Children* by Andrew Wright.

5. *Teaching Young Learners to Think: ELT Activities for Young Learners Aged 6–12* (2012) by Herbert Puchta and Marion Williams (Helbling)

   This book offers 80 ready-to-use photocopiable activities with accompanying teacher's notes. The activities themselves have been designed to promote and develop thinking skills and to develop children's language at the same time.

6. *Bringing Creative Teaching into the Young Learner Classroom* (2010) by Lynne Cameron and Penny McKay (Oxford University Press)

   If you are an inexperienced teacher, then this is a book for you. It contains 150 useful ideas and strategies that you can use in class. Each idea also has a 'Why does this work?' section, which is particularly helpful.

7. *500 Activities for the Primary Classroom* (2007) by Carol Read (Macmillan)

This book is aimed at teachers of children aged 3–12. It is a resource that will supplement the coursebook, giving plenty of varied and practical ideas to help you deal with the question: 'What on earth am I going to do in class tomorrow?'

8. *English for Primary Teachers: A Handbook of Activities & Classroom Language* (with audio CD) (2001) by Mary Slattery and Jane Willis (Oxford University Press)

This book offers practical advice and teaching suggestions to make you a confident teacher of young learners. The CD gives you examples of classroom language from real classrooms.

9. *The Primary English Teacher's Guide* (2002) by Jean Brewster, Gail Ellis and Denis Girard (Penguin Books)

This book covers the most recent developments in language-learning theories and approaches. It contains practical ideas and suggestions on a broad range of topics such as how to select materials and plan lessons for young learners and how to teach culture in the young learner classroom, and a very useful section dedicated to record-keeping and the assessment of young learners.

10. *500+ Fabulous Month-by-Month Teaching Ideas: Instant Activities and Reproducibles for Themes and Topics you Teach* (2010, Scholastic)

This book is full of practical ideas to teach children to think more deeply while learning English. It contains lots of easy-to-teach cross-curricular ideas and lessons that you can take into class to promote deeper thinking and learning. Scholastic also publishes the *Monthly Idea Book* series – one for each month – by Karen Sevaly, *40 Fabulous Social Studies Activities* by Catherine Tamblyn and *The Big Book of Quick and Easy Art Activities: More than 75 Creative Activities with Curriculum Connections* by Linda Bentley.

Unit 49

10 ELT sites and blogs

The internet has a wealth of information that can make our lives easier as teachers. The problem is finding the time to seek out the ideas that will really make a difference in your classroom. Here are 10 links that you may want to look into. Suggestions 1–5 are well-known sites that are used by teachers around the world. Suggestions 6–10 relate to blogs that will help put you in touch with other teachers and education specialists, who can have a huge impact on your teaching practices.

1. British Council

▶ Teaching English: http://www.teachingenglish.org.uk. This is a fantastic free site filled with ideas and free resources that you can take into class. It has lesson plans, school-subject-related suggestions, free webinars, ideas for teacher development and a wealth of tools that will help you put a smile on the children's faces.

▶ Learn English Kids: http://learnenglishkids.britishcouncil.org/en/. This is a fantastic site for children and their parents. It has free online games, songs, stories and activities that children can do while learning English.

2. YLTSIG (IATEFL's Young Learner Teachers' Special Interest Group)

IATEFL has various special interest groups and this is the one to join if you're teaching young learners. This site, which you can find at http://yltsig.net, will help you find out about important international events, publications and resources related to young learners.

3. Magazines for children

Both *National Geographic* and *Time Magazine* are known around the world for their quality. Both of their sites have sections that have been adapted for children. They contain engaging articles and videos to help develop children's literacy skills and general knowledge.

▶ *National Geographic for Kids*: http://kids.nationalgeographic.com (a site with fun facts, videos, photos, quizzes and lots more).

▶ *Time Magazine for Kids*: http://www.timeforkids.com (this site also has a classroom app and various printables).

4. Resources

The following sites will help you find plenty of ready-made resources to take into your classroom:

▶ **Worksheets and resources:**
http://www.twinkl.co.uk, http://www.enchantedlearning.com, http://www.esl-galaxy.com/Kids.htm, http://www.eslkidstuff.com, http://www.vanda51pro.com/, http://www.onestopenglish.com

▶ **Arts and crafts:**
http://www.dltk-kids.com

▶ **Answering children's 'Why?' questions:**
http://www.howstuffworks.com

5. Publishers' sites

You can find all sorts of ideas and free materials on the various publishers' sites, along with information about teacher development initiatives that they are holding.

- ▶ Oxford University Press's teachers' club: https://elt.oup.com/teachersclub
- ▶ Cambridge English Teacher: http://www.cambridgeenglish.org
- ▶ Macmillan Teaching Resources & Teachers' Corner: http://www.macmillanenglish.com/resources/
- ▶ Pearson's Teacher Resources: http://www.pearson.rs/teacher-s-resources.html
- ▶ Scholastic: http://www.scholastic.com/teachers/
- ▶ Express Publishing: http://www.teachers-corner.co.uk

6. Carol Read's blog: https://carolread.wordpress.com

Carol Read is a former IATEFL president and a renowned specialist on young learners. Her blog is an invaluable resource for any teacher of young learners, with lots of ideas, tips and resources that you can use.

7. Sandy Mourão's picture book blog: http://picturebooksinelt.blogspot.pt

If you're looking for a new story to read in class, then this blog is an absolute must. Here you can find story suggestions with a synopsis of each story and photos of the opening pages of the book to help you decide whether a particular storybook is suitable for your children. Sandy also has another blog with resources and tips for the young learner classroom that you want might to follow: http://sandiemourao.eu/pages/

8. Kylie Malinowska's blog: https://klokanomil.wordpress.com

This blog shares ideas to use when teaching very young learners and young learners, as well as a summary of online teacher training workshops that Kylie gives.

9. Barbara Sakamoto's blog: http://www.teachingvillage.org/

This is a great blog that is dedicated to teaching young learners. It's filled with interesting thoughts, ideas and links that will give you an idea or two to take into class the next day.

10. ETpedia blog: https://www.myetpedia.com/elt-blog/

The ETpedia concept needs no introduction. This is the blog to use when you've finished reading this book. It has lots of creative English language teaching ideas and resources to use in your classroom, and allows you to share your 10 fantastic teaching ideas with other teachers around the world.

Unit 50

Appendix

Many of the following resources can be found in colour at:
https://www.myetpedia.com/appendix-materials/

Those that are available are indicated on the page in question.

Unit 8, Introduction: Class questionnaire

Name : _____   Class: _____   Date: _____

I ♥ learning English   ☺

I like:			
learning English	☺	😐	☹
writing in the student's book or workbook	☺	😐	☹
watching videos	☺	😐	☹
listening to stories	☺	😐	☹
reading stories	☺	😐	☹
roleplaying stories	☺	😐	☹
playing with puppets	☺	😐	☹
playing games	☺	😐	☹
singing songs	☺	😐	☹
making things	☺	😐	☹
learning about the world	☺	😐	☹
speaking to my classmates in English	☺	😐	☹
doing tasks in pairs	☺	😐	☹
doing tasks in groups	☺	😐	☹
working on my own	☺	😐	☹
using a dictionary to learn English words	☺	😐	☹
using a grammar book to practise English	☺	😐	☹

 Appendix

Lesson Plan

Topic: _____	Age group: _____ Class: _____
Unit: _____	Duration of the lesson: _____
Level: _____	Lesson fit:
Date:_____	

Aims	
Main learning aims:	By the end of the lesson the children should be able to: 1. 2. 3.
Subsidiary learning aims:	1. 2.

Target language:	Vocabulary:	Grammar:

Materials:	

Unit 9, point 8: Lesson plan

Stages and procedure	Time	Interaction	On the board	Materials
Activity for fast finishers:				
Homework:				

 Appendix

Unit 10, point 3: 'Find someone who ...' bingo game

Name : _____ Class: _____ Date: _____

Write the person's name in each face.

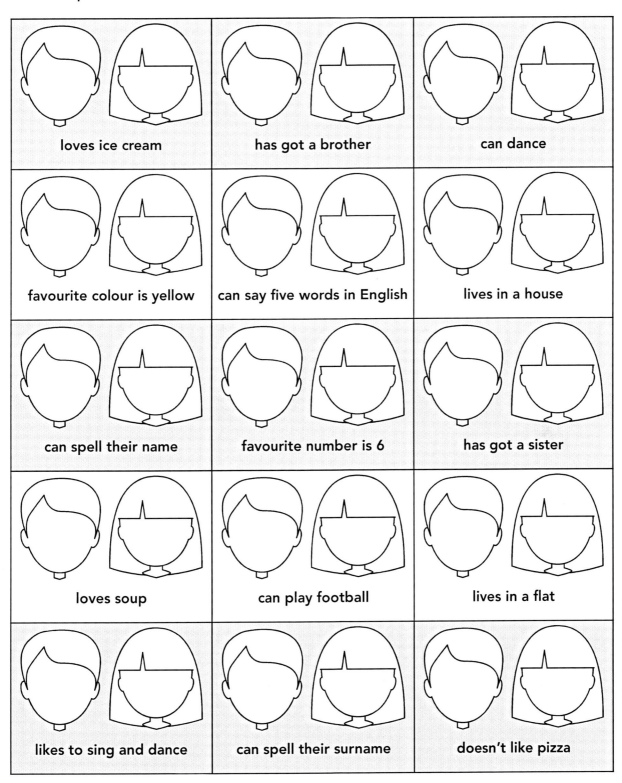

loves ice cream	has got a brother	can dance
favourite colour is yellow	can say five words in English	lives in a house
can spell their name	favourite number is 6	has got a sister
loves soup	can play football	lives in a flat
likes to sing and dance	can spell their surname	doesn't like pizza

Class : _____   Date and time: _____

| Name:_____ | Name:_____ |
| Note: | Note: |

| Name:_____ | Name:_____ |
| Note: | Note: |

aisle

aisle

Unit 12, point 9: Behaviour passport

Photo ID:

Name:

Class:

Visa: improving behaviour

Visa: improving behaviour

Visa: good behaviour

Visa: good behaviour

Visa: excellent behaviour

Visa: excellent behaviour

Appendix

Unit 13, point 10: Feedback form

Name : _____   Date: _____

1. Look and circle.

Today in class we:

I like working:

Now draw:

My favourite activity today

      Appendix

Unit 14: Common classroom instructions

Preparing to start the lesson	Vocabulary questions
1. Good morning. Please settle down. Sit down please. 2. Take out your homework. / Please give me your homework. 3. Open your books on page ..., please.	1. Please can you tell me the English word for ... 2. Does anyone know another word for.... 3. How do you say ... in English? 4. Does anyone know what you call this?

Common instructions and requests	Playing games
• I need two volunteers. • Who would like to volunteer to ...? • Work in pairs/groups please. • Take turns to ... • Sit facing your partner. • Swap/exchange papers with your partner. • Please help each other. • Don't let your partner see your work/cards. • Close/open the window please. • Listen carefully. • Please collect all your books and put them on my table. • Please give out the worksheets. • Please tidy up. • Please put away your books. • Come to the board please. • Put your hand up please. • Listen and colour in. • Copy the words on the board.	• Let's play a game which... • Look and find what is missing. • Jumble the letters. • Order the letters and discover the secret word. • A point for this team. • Remember, no cheating. • Sorry, you are out. • Try again please. • Congratulations. You won! • Throw the dice. • Now it's your turn. • Miss a turn. • Find the matching pair. • Listen to your partner and... • Shuffle the cards. • Throw the dice. • Place the cards face down. • Pick a card. • Choose a card. • Turn a card over.

Numbering	Reprimanding
• Write the numbers 1 to 10 in the margin. • Order the pictures. • What's first? What's next? What's last?	• I think that you can do a bit/even better than this. Please try again! • If you choose to continue ... then you also choose to ... • We said that we would use a whispering voice. Is that a whispering voice? • Do you think that you are respecting our class rules? What happens when you don't ...?

Checking understanding	Giving encouragement
• Can anyone explain what you have to do? • Please tell me what you have to do. • Please put your hand up if you know the answer.	• Well done. • That's nearly right. Why don't you try again? • Good/great job!

Appendix

Unit 14: Common classroom instructions

Checking understanding	Giving encouragement
• Are you going to … or are you going to …? • What do we do next? • Show me … / Point to … • Clap your hands if you think this is correct and stamp your feet if you think that is wrong.	• Excellent!/Well done! • That's it! Keep on trying. • Good try! High five! • Congratulations! • Easy, peasy, lemon squeezy (to show that something is really easy).
Setting homework	**Ending the lesson**
• For homework please do Exercise … on page …. • What's your homework? • What page is your homework on? • What do you have to do in Exercise 1?	• Please put your books away. It's time to tidy up. • Well done, everyone! I'm so proud of you. • See you tomorrow/next time. • Let's sing the Goodbye Song.

 Appendix

Unit 15, point 4: Challenge of the day: riddles

Riddle	Answer
What goes up when rain comes down?	An umbrella.
What can you catch but not throw?	A cold.
What kind of tree can you carry in your hand?	A palm.
What has one eye but cannot see?	A needle.
How many months have 28 days?	All the months (they all have at least 28 days).
What goes up but never comes down?	Your age.
What is at the end of a rainbow?	The letter W.
What is always coming but never arrives?	Tomorrow.
What has a neck but no head?	A bottle.
What can you hear but not touch or see?	Your voice.

Jeopardy template

(Also Unit 17, Point 8)

1. Choose the topics that you want the children to answer questions on, for example:
   Topic 1: guess the word (mime a word for the class to guess).
   Topic 2: spell a word (show the children a flashcard and they have to spell that word).
   Topic 3: say a word (show the children a flashcard and they have to say that word).
   Topic 4: make a sentence with a word (give the children a word and they have to make a sentence with that word).
   Topic 5: draw a word (say a word and the children have to draw it).
2. Next, choose five words for each topic. Make sure that you choose words which progress in level of difficulty.
3. Divide the children into two teams. Each team rolls a dice. Whichever team gets the highest number goes first. That team chooses a box on the Jeopardy board. If they guess the word correctly, they win the money in that box. Then the other team has a go. The team with the most money at the end (ie when all the boxes have been won) is the winner.

Topic 1	Topic 2	Topic 3	Topic 4	Topic 5
$100	$100	$100	$100	$100
$200	$200	$200	$200	$200
$300	$300	$300	$300	$300
$400	$400	$400	$400	$400
$500	$500	$500	$500	$500

Unit 15, point 8: Self-evaluation form

Name:

About me:

I follow my teacher's instructions.	☺	😐	☹
I am a good listener.	☺	😐	☹
I am a good friend.	☺	😐	☹
I am responsible.	☺	😐	☹
I do my work on time.	☺	😐	☹
I try my best.	☺	😐	☹

About my work:

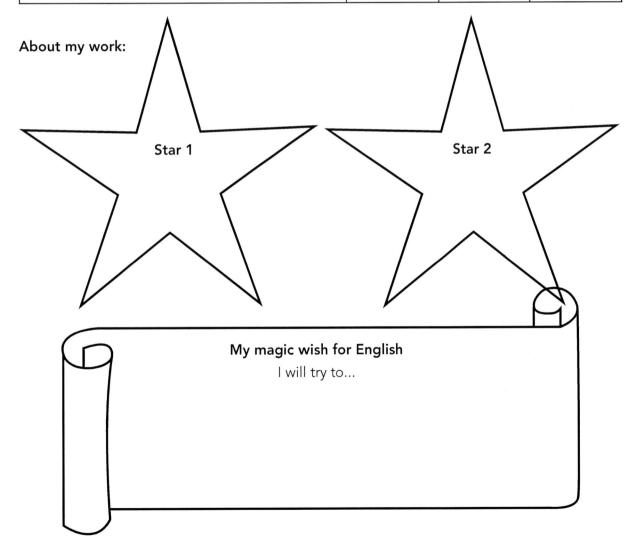

Star 1

Star 2

My magic wish for English
I will try to...

Unit 16, point 3; Unit 42, point 9: Survey template

Name : _____   Class: _____   Date: _____

Survey question:_____

Number of people						
	10					
	9					
	8					
	7					
	6					
	5					
	4					
	3					
	2					
	1					

_____ _____ _____ _____ _____

Number of people interviewed

I interviewed _____ people.

Survey feedback

_____ people like _____

_____ people like _____

_____ people like _____

_____ people like _____

_____ people like _____

Main conclusions

This survey allows me to say that _____

_____

_____

     Appendix

Unit 16, point 8: Read and draw

A full colour version of this material is available at https://www.myetpedia.com/appendix-materials/

1. A monster

Can you draw my monster? Let's try. My monster has got a small round body. Yes, that's right. My monster has got a small round body. Please draw a small round body. Finished? My monster has got a big square head. That's right. My monster has got a big square head. Now, let's draw his arms. Are you ready? My monster has got four arms. Two on the left and two on the right. That's four arms. Now, let's draw his legs. My monster has got two long, thin legs. That's right. My monster has got two long, thin legs. Now, look at his face. My monster has got three eyes. Two are small and one is big. That's right. My monster has got two small eyes and one big eye. What colour is my monster? That's easy! My monster is your favourite colour!

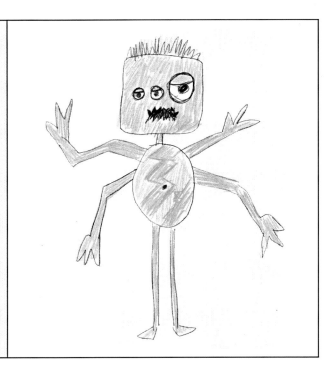

2. Your best friend

Let's draw your best friend today. That's right. Today we are going to draw your best friend today. Let's draw their head. That's right. Please draw their head. Ready. Now, let's draw their hair. Please draw your best friend's hair now. What colour is your best friend's hair? Please colour in their hair. Finished? That's great! Now, let's draw your best friend's eyes. That's right. Please draw their eyes. What colour are your best friend's eyes? Please colour in their eyes. Time to draw your best friend's mouth. Ready? Is the mouth big or small? Please draw your best friend's mouth now. Ready to draw your best friend's body? Is your best friend short or tall? And is your best friend fat or thin? Please draw your best friend's body now. Remember to draw their clothes. What clothes do they like wearing? Please draw the clothes they like wearing. What's your best friend's name? Please write your best friend's name under your drawing. That's right. Please write your best friend's name under your drawing. That's just perfect!

3. My house

Can you draw my house? Let's try. I've got a big house. It has got two floors: the ground floor and the first floor. Yes, that's right. My house has got two floors: the ground floor and the first floor.

Now, let's draw the ground floor. Great! First, let's draw a big kitchen. That's right. Please draw a big kitchen. Finished? Now, next to the kitchen, please draw a small dining room. Yes, a small dining room. Please draw a small dining room. Finished? Now let's draw the sitting room. I have got a big sitting room. The sitting room in my house is big and it is next to the dining room.

Ready? Now, let's draw the first floor of my house. The first floor is above the ground floor. My bedroom is on the first floor. It is very big. Yes, that's right. My bedroom is on the first floor and it is very big. There is a small bathroom next to my bedroom. Yes, that's right. The bathroom in my house is small and it's next to my bedroom. Finished? Now, let's draw the study. I have got a study. It's next to the bathroom. Yes, that's right. The study is small and it's next to my bathroom.

Ready to draw the garden? There is a small garden in front of my house. Can you draw a small garden in front of my house? That's right. Please draw a small garden in front of my house. There are two big trees in my garden. Please draw two big trees in my garden. There are lots of flowers in my garden. Can you draw lots of flowers in my garden? That's right. Please draw lots of flowers in my garden. I love my house!

Vocabulary chase

How to play

1. Choose 36 flashcards of vocabulary that the children have learnt. You should have a different flashcard for each square on the grid.
2. Put numbered sticky notes (1–36) on the back of the flashcards – one sticky note per flashcard. Then lay them out number-side-up next to the board.
3. Put the children into groups and get them to roll the dice. The group with the highest number goes first.
4. The groups take turns to roll the dice and move their counters accordingly. If they throw a three, for example, they move their counter three squares along the grid.
5. The number they land on corresponds to the flashcard with that number on it. They must find the flashcard, turn it over and identify the vocabulary item. If they do so correctly, they get to stay in that box. If not, they have to move back to the previous box they were in.
6. The winner is the first group to get to the last box.

36	35	34	33	32	31
25	26	27	28	29	30
24	23	22	21	20	19
13	14	15	16	17	18
12	11	10	9	8	7
1	2	3	4	5	6

Noughts and crosses

(Also Unit 44, Point 10)

> This games can be played as a class or in pairs.
> 1. Get the children to make at least 9 mini-flashcards on the topic you are teaching, eg clothes (see the mini-flashcard template for Unit 33, Point 6).
> 2. The children put the cards face down on the table and shuffle them around.
> 3. They then put them face down on the noughts-and-crosses board without turning them over or seeing what's on the other side.
> 4. Each child rolls a dice. Whoever rolls the highest number goes first. He or she chooses which symbol to play with: X or O.
> 5. The first child to play chooses a square and turns the card over. If the child is able to say the word, he or she is allowed to keep the card, placing their symbol card there instead.
> 6. Then it is the next child's turn. The first child to make a row of noughts or crosses is the winner.

ETpedia: Young Learners © Pavilion Publishing and Media Ltd and its licensors 2016. **Appendix**

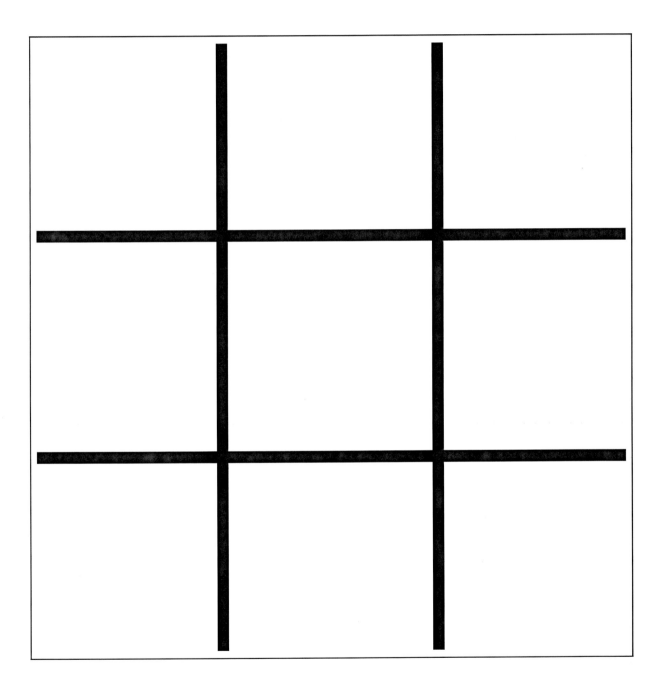

Name : _____   Class: _____   Date: _____

The print letters of the alphabet

Aa		Bb		Cc	
Dd		Ee		Ff	
Gg		Hh		Ii	
Jj		Kk		Ll	
Mm		Nn		Oo	
Pp		Qq		Rr	
Ss		Tt		Uu	
Vv		Ww		Xx	
Yy		Zz			

Name : _____ Class: _____ Date: _____

The cursive letters of the alphabet

Aa		*Bb*		*Cc*	
Dd		*Ee*		*Ff*	
Gg		*Hh*		*Ii*	
Jj		*Kk*		*Ll*	
Mm		*Nn*		*Oo*	
Pp		*Qq*		*Rr*	
Ss		*Tt*		*Uu*	
Vv		*Ww*		*Xx*	
Yy		*Zz*			

Name : _____ **Class:** _____ **Date:** _____

A is for **a**pple and **A**nt

1. Practise writing this letter and say its name.

   Aa Aa /a/ apple /a/ ant

2. Trace the lowercase letters.

3. Now write the lowercase letters several times.

4. Trace the uppercase letters.

5. Now write the uppercase letters several times.

6. Trace the sentence.

   Ants like to eat apples.

7. Now write the sentence several times.

 Appendix

Unit 21: Song lyrics

Please check how to sing the tunes on YouTube.

1. Head, Shoulders, Knees and Toes

1. Head and shoulders knees and toes
   Knees and toes
   Head and shoulders knees and toes
   Knees and toes
   And eyes and ears
   And mouth and nose
   Head and shoulders knees and toes
   Knees and toes

2. Feet and tummies arms and chins
   Arms and chins
   Feet and tummies arms and chins
   Arms and chins
   And eyes and ears
   And mouth and shins
   Feet and tummies arms and chins
   Arms and chins

3. Hands and fingers legs and lips
   Legs and lips
   Hands and fingers legs and lips
   Legs and lips
   And eyes and ears
   And mouth and hips
   Hands and fingers legs and lips
   Legs and lips

   [Repeat first verse]

2. The Hokey Cokey

1. You put your right arm in,
   your right arm out
   In, out, in, out,
   You shake it all about.
   You do the Hokey Cokey and you turn around
   That's what it's all about!

   [Chorus]
   Woah, the Hokey Cokey,
   Woah, the Hokey Cokey,
   Woah, the Hokey Cokey,
   Knees bent, arms stretched, rah rah rah!

2. You put your left arm in,
   your left arm out
   In, out, in, out,
   You shake it all about.
   You do the Hokey Cokey and you turn around
   That's what it's all about!

   [Chorus]

3. You put your right leg in,
   your right leg out
   In, out, in, out,
   You shake it all about.
   You do the Hokey Cokey and you turn around
   That's what it's all about!

   [Chorus]

4. You put your left leg in,
   your left leg out
   In, out, in, out,
   You shake it all about.
   You do the Hokey Cokey and you turn around
   That's what it's all about!

   All together now
   [Chorus]

5. You put your whole self in,
   your whole self out
   In, out, in, out,
   You shake it all about.
   You do the Hokey Cokey and you turn around
   That's what it's all about!

     ETpedia: Young Learners © Pavilion Publishing and Media Ltd and its licensors 2016.   **Appendix**

3. The Colours of the Rainbow

The colours of the rainbow are red and orange, red and orange, red and orange,
The colours of the rainbow are red and orange,
In the grey sky.
The colours of the rainbow are yellow, green and blue, …

The colours of the rainbow are indigo and violet, …

4. If You're Happy and You Know It

1. If you're happy and you know it, clap your hands (clap clap)
   If you're happy and you know it, clap your hands (clap clap)
   If you're happy and you know it, then your face will surely show it
   If you're happy and you know it, clap your hands. (clap clap)

2. If you're happy and you know it, stomp your feet (stomp stomp)
   If you're happy and you know it, stomp your feet (stomp stomp)
   If you're happy and you know it, then your face will surely show it
   If you're happy and you know it, stomp your feet. (stomp stomp)

3. If you're happy and you know it, shout 'Hurray!' (hoo-ray!)
   If you're happy and you know it, shout 'Hurray!' (hoo-ray!)
   If you're happy and you know it, then your face will surely show it
   If you're happy and you know it, shout 'Hurray!' (hoo-ray!)

4. If you're happy and you know it, do all three (clap-clap, stomp-stomp, hoo-ray!)
   If you're happy and you know it, do all three (clap-clap, stomp-stomp, hoo-ray!)
   If you're happy and you know it, then your face will surely show it
   If you're happy and you know it, do all three. (clap-clap, stomp-stomp, hoo-ray!)

5. Do You Like Broccoli Ice Cream?

1. Do you like broccoli?
   Yes, I do! [Yes gesture.]
   Do you like ice cream? [Pretend to lick an ice cream cone.]
   Yes, I do! [Yes gesture.]
   Do you like broccoli ice cream? [Make a 'yucky' face.]
   No, I don't. Yucky! [No gesture.]

2. Do you like doughnuts? [Pretend to hold and eat a doughnut.]
   Yes, I do!
   Do you like juice? [Pretend to drink juice.]
   Yes, I do!
   Do you like doughnut juice?
   No, I don't. Yucky!

3. Do you like popcorn? [Pretend to eat popcorn.]
   Yes, I do!
   Do you like pizza? [Pretend to hold a piece of pizza and eat it.]
   Yes, I do!
   Do you like popcorn pizza?
   No, I don't. Yucky!

4. Do you like bananas? [Pretend to peel and eat a banana.]
   Yes, I do!
   Do you like soup? [Pretend to eat soup from a bowl with a spoon.]
   Yes, I do!
   Do you like banana soup?
   No, I don't. Yuck!

6. The Wheels on the Bus

1. The wheels on the bus go round and round,
   round and round,
   round and round.
   The wheels on the bus go round and round,
   all through the town.

2. The wipers on the bus go swish, swish, swish;
   swish, swish, swish;
   swish, swish, swish.
   The wipers on the bus go swish, swish, swish,
   all through the town.

3. The horn on the bus goes beep, beep, beep;
   beep, beep, beep;
   beep, beep, beep.
   The horn on the bus goes beep, beep, beep,
   all through the town.

4. The money on the bus goes clink, clink, clink;
   clink, clink, clink;
   clink, clink, clink.
   The money on the bus goes clink, clink, clink,
   all through the town.

5. The driver on the bus says, 'Move along please,
   move along please, move along please'.
   The driver on the bus says, 'Move on back',
   all through the town.

6. The baby on the bus says, 'Wah, wah, wah;
   Wah, wah, wah;
   Wah, wah, wah'.
   The baby on the bus says 'Wah, wah, wah',
   all through the town.

7. The mummy on the bus says, 'Shush, shush, shush;
   shush, shush, shush;
   shush, shush, shush'.
   The mummy on the bus says, 'Shush, shush, shush',
   all through the town.

7. Incy Wincy Spider

Incy Wincy Spider, climbing up the spout
Down came the rain and washed the spider out
Out came the sun and dried up all the rain
Now Incy Wincy Spider went up the spout again!

8. Old Macdonald Had a Farm

1. Old Macdonald had a farm
E-I-E-I-O
And on his farm he had a cow
E-I-E-I-O
With a moo moo here
And a moo moo there
Here a moo, there a moo
Everywhere a moo moo
Old Macdonald had a farm
E-I-E-I-O

2. Old Macdonald had a farm
E-I-E-I-O
And on his farm he had a pig
E-I-E-I-O
With an oink oink here
And an oink oink there
Here an oink, there an oink
Everywhere an oink oink
With a moo moo here
And a moo moo there
Here a moo, there a moo
Everywhere a moo moo
Old Macdonald had a farm
E-I-E-I-O

3. ... And on his farm he had a duck
E-I-E-I-O
With a quack quack here ...

4. ... Andd on his farm he had a horse
E-I-E-I-O
With a neigh neigh here ...

5. ... And on his farm he had a lamb
E-I-E-I-O
With a baa baa here ...

6. ... And on his farm he had some chickens
E-I-E-I-O
With a cluck cluck here ...

7. Old Macdonald had a farm
E-I-E-I-OOOOOOO.

9. Five Little Monkeys

1. Five little monkeys jumping on the bed
One fell off and bumped his head
Mama called the doctor,
And the doctor said
No more monkeys jumping on the bed!

2. Four little monkeys jumping on the bed ...

3. Three little monkeys jumping on the bed ...

4. Two little monkeys jumping on the bed ...

5. One little monkey jumping on the bed
One fell off and bumped his head
Mama called the doctor
And the doctor said,
Put that monkey right to bed!

10. The Alphabet Song

A - B - C - D - E - F - G
H - I - J - K - L - M - N - O - P
Q - R - S - T - U - V,
W - X - Y and Z
Now I know my ABCs
Next time, won't you sing with me?

Song name:_____

1. Ask your question (Do you like [name of song]?)
   Then colour in the graph.

10			
9			
8			
7			
6			
5			
4			
3			
2			
1			

☺   😐   ☹

2. Analyse your answers and draw a conclusion:

Number of people interviewed

I interviewed _____ people.

Survey feedback

_____ people said that they like the song.

_____ people said that the song is OK.

_____ people said that they don't like the song.

I _____ the song.

Conclusion

This survey shows that my friends mostly _____the song we sang in class today.

Unit 25: Fun rhymes

1. Twinkle, Twinkle, Little Star

1. Twinkle, twinkle, little star,
   How I wonder what you are!
   Up above the world so high,
   Like a diamond in the sky.
   Twinkle, twinkle, little star,
   How I wonder what you are!

2. When the blazing sun is gone,
   When he nothing shines upon,
   Then you show your little light,
   Twinkle, twinkle, all the night.
   Twinkle, twinkle, little star,
   How I wonder what you are!

3. Then the traveller in the dark,
   Thanks you for your tiny spark,
   He could not see which way to go,
   If you did not twinkle so.
   Twinkle, twinkle, little star,
   How I wonder what you are!

4. In the dark blue sky you keep,
   And often through my curtains peep,
   For you never shut your eye,
   Till the sun is in the sky.
   Twinkle, twinkle, little star,
   How I wonder what you are!

5. As your bright and tiny spark,
   Lights the traveller in the dark,
   Though I know not what you are,
   Twinkle, twinkle, little star.
   Twinkle, twinkle, little star,
   How I wonder what you are!

2. Humpty Dumpty

Humpty Dumpty sat on a wall,
Humpty Dumpty had a great fall;
All the king's horses and all the king's men
Couldn't put Humpty together again.

3. Baa Baa Black Sheep

1. Baa, baa, black sheep, have you any wool?
   Yes sir, yes sir, three bags full!
   One for the master,
   One for the dame,
   And one for the little boy
   Who lives down the lane.

2. Baa, baa, white sheep, have you any wool?
   Yes sir, yes sir, three needles full.
   One to mend a jumper,
   One to mend a frock,
   And one for the little girl
   With holes in her sock.

3. Baa, baa, grey sheep, have you any wool?
   Yes sir, yes sir, three bags full.
   One for the kitten,
   One for the cats,
   And one for the owner
   To knit some woolly hats.

4. Baa, baa, bare sheep, have you any wool?
   No sir, no sir, no bags full.
   None for the master,
   None for the dame,
   And none for the little boy
   who lives down the lane.

4. Jack and Jill

1. Jack and Jill went up the hill
   To fetch a pail of water.
   Jack fell down and broke his crown,
   And Jill came tumbling after.

2. Up Jack got, and home did trot,
   As fast as he could caper,
   He went to bed to mend his head,
   With vinegar and brown paper.

5. Hickory Dickory Dock

1. Hickory Dickory Dock,
   The mouse ran up the clock,
   The clock struck one,
   The mouse ran down! *Hickory Dickory Dock.*

2. Hickory Dickory Dock,
   The bird looked at the clock,
   The clock struck two,
   Away she flew! *Hickory Dickory Dock.*

3. Hickory Dickory Dock,
   The dog barked at the clock,
   The clock struck three,
   Fiddle de dee! *Hickory Dickory Dock.*

4. Hickory Dickory Dock,
   The bear slept by the clock,
   The clock struck four,
   He ran out the door! *Hickory Dickory Dock.*

5. Hickory Dickory Dock,
   The bee buzzed round the clock,
   The clock struck five,
   She went to her hive! *Hickory Dickory Dock.*

6. Hickory Dickory Dock,
   The hen pecked at the clock,
   The clock struck six,
   Oh, fiddle-sticks,
   Hickory Dickory Dock!

Unit 27, point 2: Example of visual storytelling plan

A full colour version of this material is available at https://www.myetpedia.com/appendix-materials/

(based on *Silly Sally* by Audrey Wood)

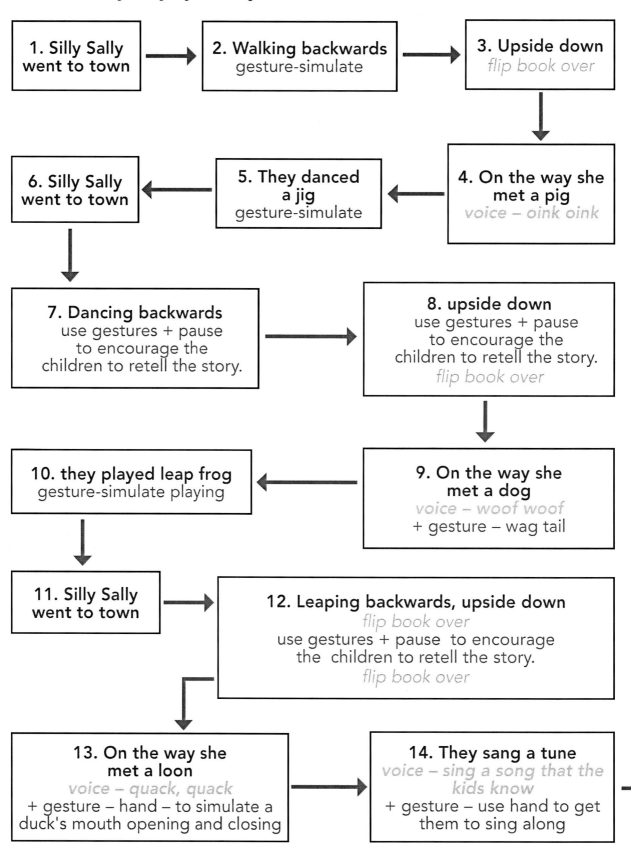

| 1. Silly Sally went to town | → | 2. Walking backwards
gesture-simulate | → | 3. Upside down
flip book over |

| 6. Silly Sally went to town | ← | 5. They danced a jig
gesture-simulate | ← | 4. On the way she met a pig
voice – oink oink |

7. Dancing backwards
use gestures + pause to encourage the children to retell the story.

8. upside down
use gestures + pause to encourage the children to retell the story.
flip book over

10. they played leap frog
gesture-simulate playing

9. On the way she met a dog
voice – woof woof
+ gesture – wag tail

11. Silly Sally went to town

12. Leaping backwards, upside down
flip book over
use gestures + pause to encourage the children to retell the story.
flip book over

13. On the way she met a loon
voice – quack, quack
+ gesture – hand – to simulate a duck's mouth opening and closing

14. They sang a tune
voice – sing a song that the kids know
+ gesture – use hand to get them to sing along

Appendix

Unit 27, point 2: Example of visual storytelling plan

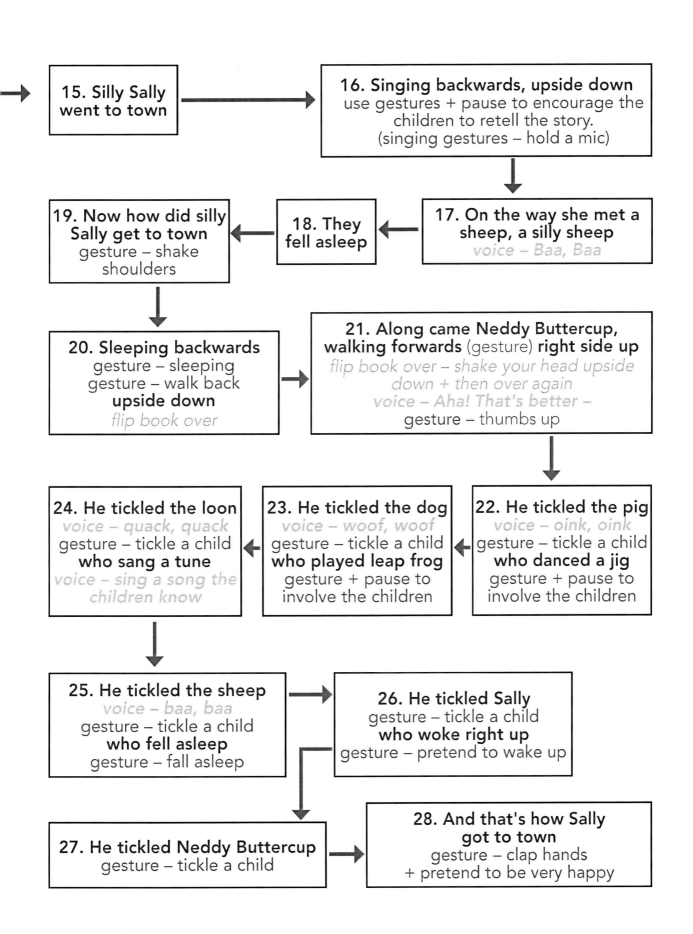

15. Silly Sally went to town

16. Singing backwards, upside down
use gestures + pause to encourage the children to retell the story.
(singing gestures – hold a mic)

17. On the way she met a sheep, a silly sheep
voice – Baa, Baa

18. They fell asleep

19. Now how did silly Sally get to town
gesture – shake shoulders

20. Sleeping backwards
gesture – sleeping
gesture – walk back
upside down
flip book over

21. Along came Neddy Buttercup, walking forwards (gesture) **right side up**
flip book over – shake your head upside down + then over again
voice – Aha! That's better –
gesture – thumbs up

22. He tickled the pig
voice – oink, oink
gesture – tickle a child
who danced a jig
gesture + pause to involve the children

23. He tickled the dog
voice – woof, woof
gesture – tickle a child
who played leap frog
gesture + pause to involve the children

24. He tickled the loon
voice – quack, quack
gesture – tickle a child
who sang a tune
voice – sing a song the children know

25. He tickled the sheep
voice – baa, baa
gesture – tickle a child
who fell asleep
gesture – fall asleep

26. He tickled Sally
gesture – tickle a child
who woke right up
gesture – pretend to wake up

27. He tickled Neddy Buttercup
gesture – tickle a child

28. And that's how Sally got to town
gesture – clap hands
+ pretend to be very happy

A full colour version of this material is available at https://www.myetpedia.com/appendix-materials/

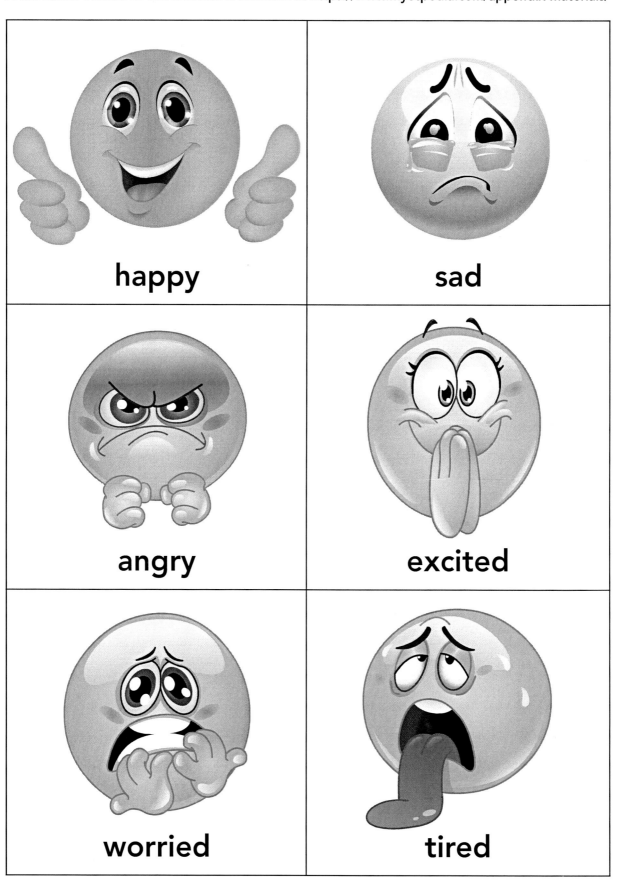

happy

sad

angry

excited

worried

tired

 Appendix

hungry

hot

cold

sleepy

Rules for playing a game with the fortune-teller

Child 1 invites Child 2 to choose a colour.

Child 2 chooses a colour on the fortune-teller.

Child 1 spells the colour that Child 2 has chosen and opens and closes the fortune-teller with each letter.

Child 1 invites Child 2 to choose a number.

Child 2 chooses a number on the fortune-teller.

Child 1 lifts that number and reads out the question for Child 2 to answer.

Child 2 answers the question.

Play again.

Suggested questions for the fortune-teller

What's your name?

What's your surname?

What's your favourite toy?

How do you spell 'pencil'?

What's your favourite number?

What's your favourite colour?

What's your favourite food and drink?

How do you spell 'eight'?

Unit 32, point 6: Finger puppets

A full colour version of this material is available at https://www.myetpedia.com/appendix-materials/

Materials needed:
1. old rubber gloves
2. ribbon/wool for the hair
3. plastic eyes
4. permanent markers and glitter glue to decorate the puppets
5. bits of old fabric for the clothes
6. liquid glue to stick on the decorations

Instructions:
1. Take the rubber glove and cut the fingers at the base.
2. Make the hair and stick it on. Glue on the eyes and the clothes. Allow the glue to dry.
3. Draw the eyes and mouth with the glitter glue or permanent markers and allow to dry.
4. Decorate the clothes with glitter glue.

Step 1: Cut out the template along the dotted lines.

Step 2: Fold the template to form a cube.

Step 3: Glue the flaps and stick the edges of the dice together.

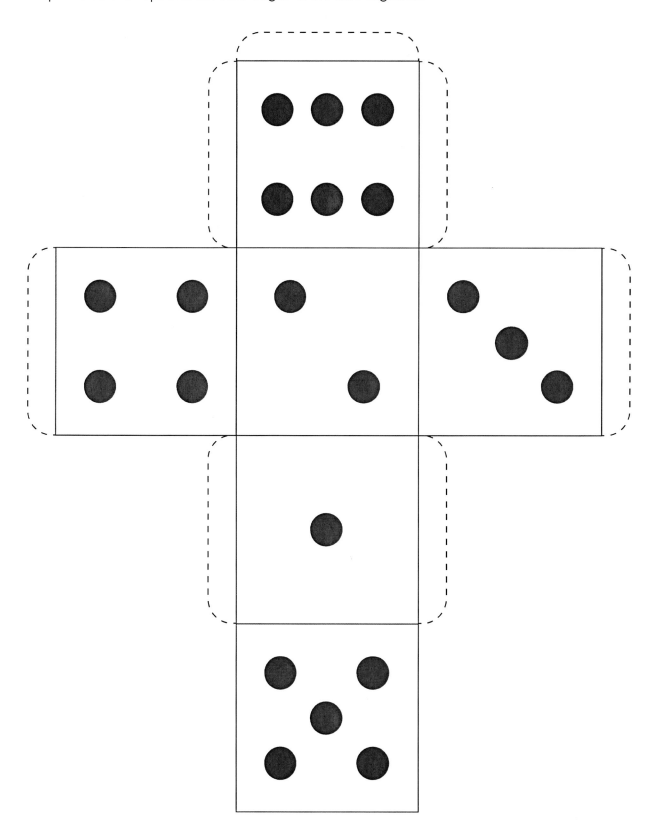

Adaptation for story/house dice

1. To make a story dice, use the blank dice template below and either:
   a. draw/stick an image of a main character/event of the story on each square of the dice

   OR

   a. write a key word from the story in each square.

Make sure that each square has only one image or word on it.

2. The children roll the dice and have to:
   a. tell the story from the point of view of that character
   b. say what happens to that character, or what happens in that event in the story
   c. answer questions about that particular character/event

Appendix

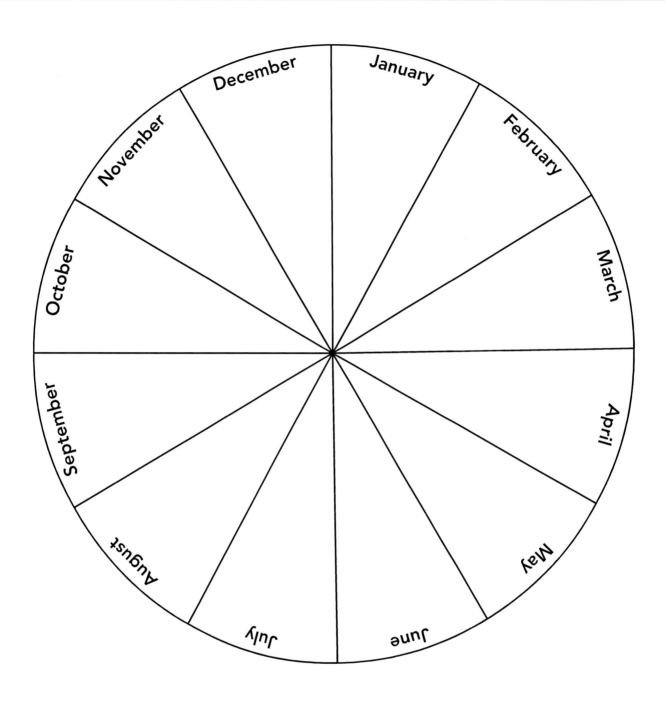

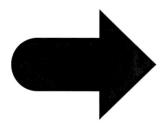

 Appendix

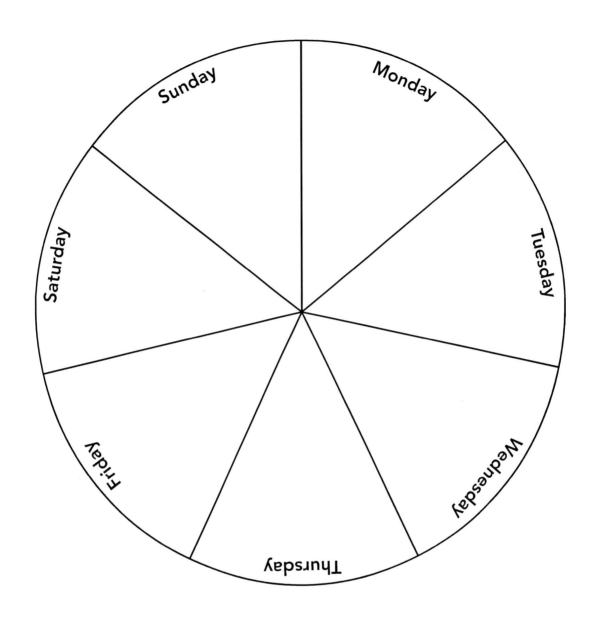

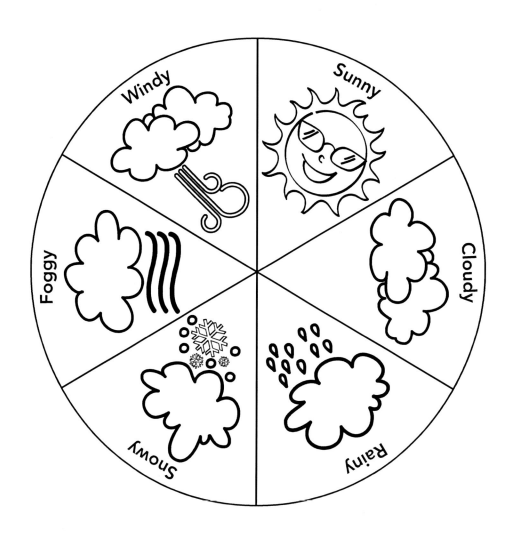

 Appendix

What time is it?

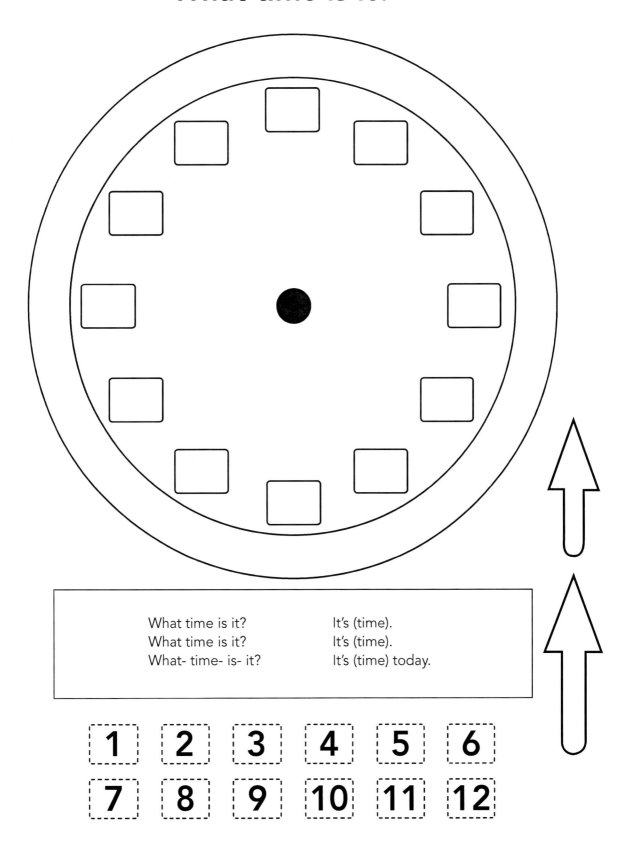

What time is it?	It's (time).
What time is it?	It's (time).
What- time- is- it?	It's (time) today.

Unit 33, point 4: Topic spinner

Instructions:

1. Draw a picture or write a word in each section and colour it in.
2. Cut out the spinner.
3. Stick the spinner on a sheet of strong cardboard.
4. Punch the centre hole with a pencil. Spin the wheel and start to play.

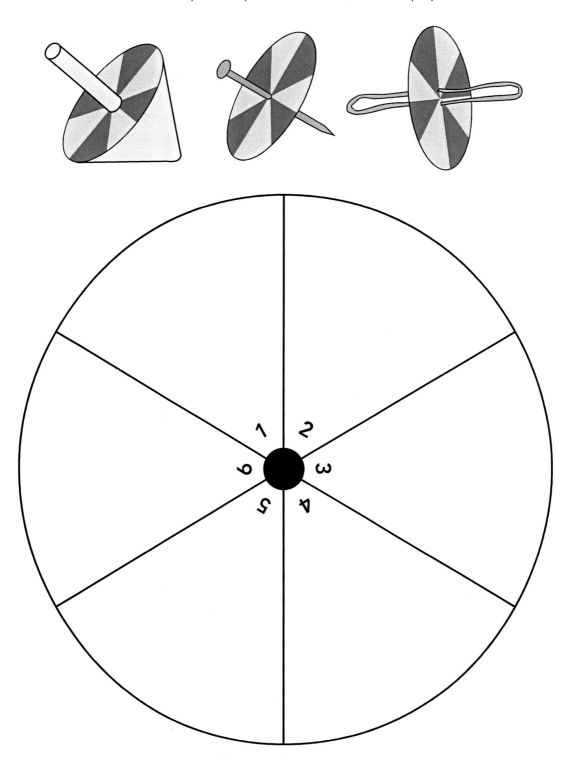

ETpedia: Young Learners © Pavilion Publishing and Media Ltd and its licensors 2016.   **Appendix**

Appendix

Unit 33, point 7: Topic wheel
Unit 40, point 3: Body wheel

Instructions:
1. Cut out both circles along the outer dark lines.
2. Take the circle with the notch cut out of it and write the topic of the vocabulary that you want to work on, eg 'The Body'.
3. Take the circle with the numbers on it and write a word for each number on the right side of the circle for the topic chosen, eg 1. arm 2. head, etc. Draw a picture for each word on the other side of the circle in the corresponding number section.
4. Place the circle with the window on top of this circle and attach both circles with a brass fastener in the centre of the black circle.
5. The children test their vocabulary by looking at a picture and saying the word. Then they move the circle and check the word section to see whether they were right.

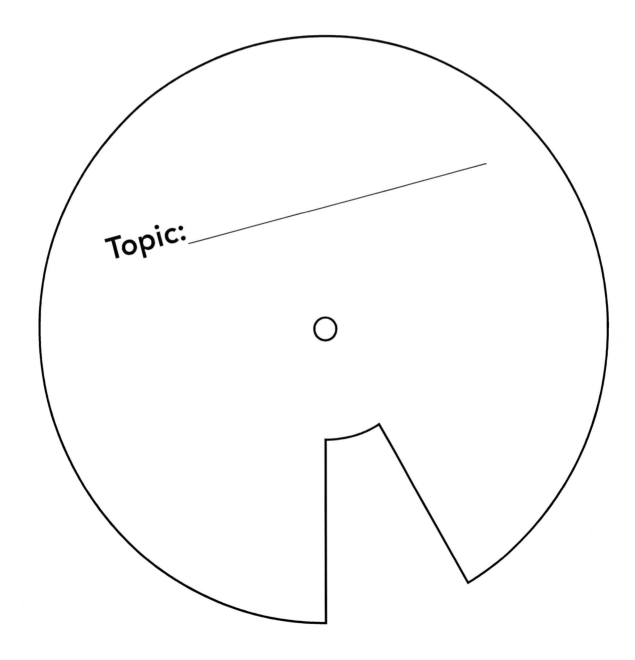

Appendix

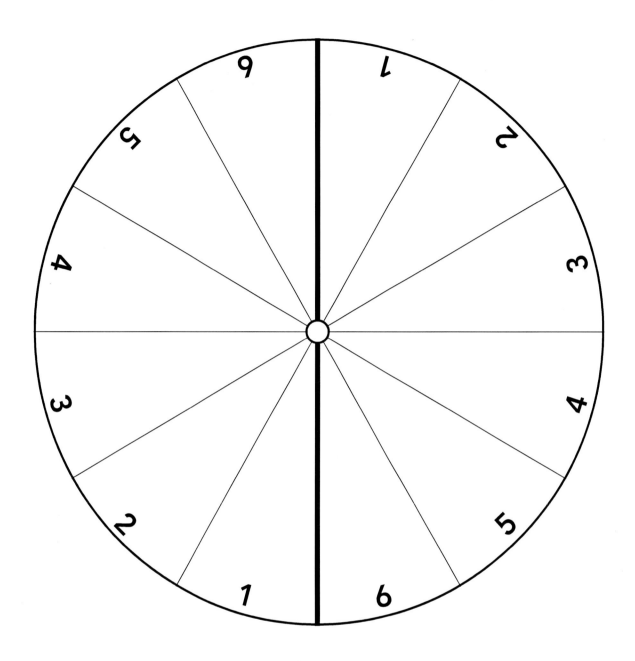

ETpedia: Young Learners © Pavilion Publishing and Media Ltd and its licensors 2016. **Appendix**

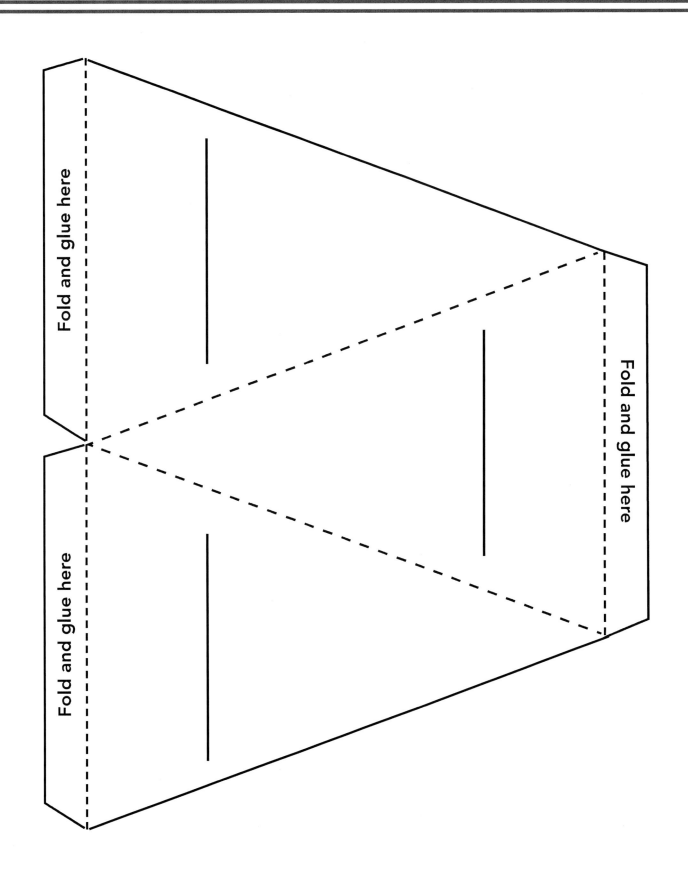

Front:

My Crazy Sentence Machine						

Back:

Glue here on the inside		Glue here on the inside		Glue here on the inside		Glue here on the inside

Sentence strips:

I	have got		tennis
You	has got		the ball
He	am		a car
She	is		a girl
We	are		sing
They	can		happy
It	like		the piano
They	play		pizza

Unit 33, point 9: Crazy sentence-maker

Blank template for children to create their own sentence-maker using words they have learnt for any particular topic:

Unit 37, point 4: Hungry monster

Name : _____   Class: _____   Date: _____

My hungry monster

1. Choose and cut out *only the healthy snacks*. Then feed the hungry monster.

Name : _____ Class: _____ Date: _____

1. Look at the key and colour in the rainbow.

1	2	3	4	5	6	7
yellow	red	blue	green	orange	indigo	violet

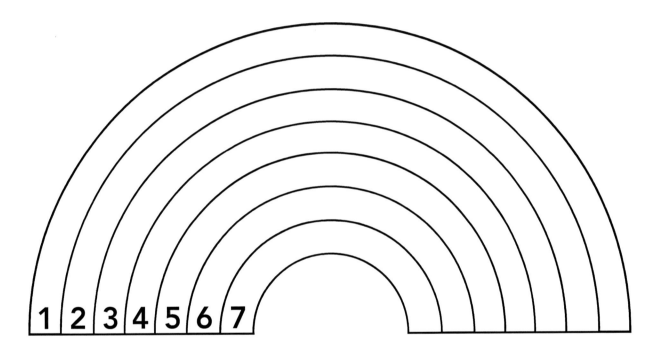

A full colour version of this material is available at https://www.myetpedia.com/appendix-materials/

Materials needed

1. thick cardboard
2. coloured paper
3. coloured crepe paper
4. scissors
5. liquid glue
6. markers
7. string

Instructions

1. Draw the outline of a big fish on the thick cardboard and cut it out. Draw the details (eyes, scales, etc.) of the fish in pencil.
2. Cut out 3–5 strips of different coloured crepe paper and glue them on the end of the fish's tail.
3. Using the coloured paper, cut out different-coloured scales and glue them onto the fish starting from the end of the tail and moving towards the head. Remember to cover the strips of crepe paper near the fish's tail with coloured scales, too, so that you don't notice where you have glued them.
4. Colour in the head and cut out an eye for the fish. Glue it on the head.
5. Use a marker to outline the different parts of the fish.
6. Follow steps 3–5 to decorate the other side of the fish.
7. Make a small hole near the fish's mouth and attach the string so that you can hang it up.

 Appendix

How to make an animal strip book:

1. Photocopy a 'book pages' template for each page that you'd like the children to have (four pages = four handouts)
2. The children draw a different animal on each page as follows:

   Rectangle 1: the animal's head

   Rectangle 2: the animal's body

   Rectangle 3: The animal's legs

3. Join all the pages together. Then add a front and back cover, which the children decorate in the frames provided.
4. Attach all the pages with brass fasteners or staples.
5. The children cut out the strips along the dotted lines.
6. The children make the front and back covers.
7. The children invent a crazy animal by choosing a different strip for each animal body part.

Book pages:

Unit 38, point 4: Crazy animal strip book

Back cover:

This book is about:

____

____

____

____

Keywords:

____

____

Front cover:

Title: ______________________________

Author: ______________________________

Name: _____ Class: _____ Date: _____

Venn Diagram

Topic:

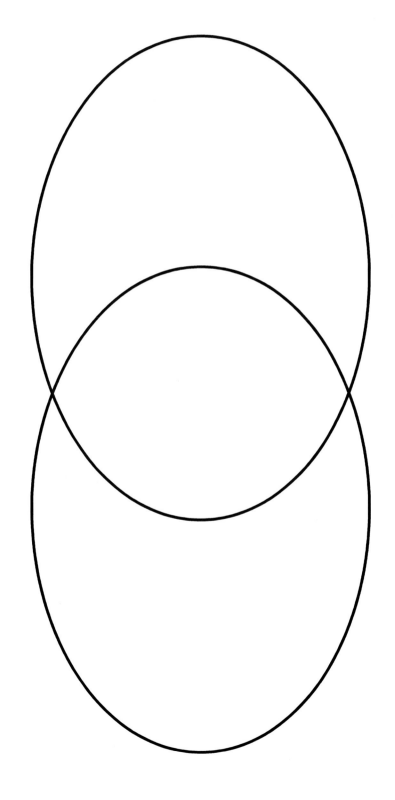

ETpedia: Young Learners © Pavilion Publishing and Media Ltd and its licensors 2016. **197**

A full colour version of this material is available at https://www.myetpedia.com/appendix-materials/

Look and play bingo

BINGO			

A full colour version of this material is available at https://www.myetpedia.com/appendix-materials/

Step 1: Give a blank copy of the jigsaw template (see below) to each child. Alternatively, use these ready-made toy flashcards.

Step 2: The children draw and colour in pictures of their favourite toys.

Step 3: Stick the jigsaw on a piece of cardboard.

Step 4: The children cut out the pieces.

Step 5: Give each child an envelope. They write their name on it and decorate it.

Step 6: The children put the pieces of their puzzles in the envelope.

Step 7: The children swap jigsaws and do each other's puzzles.

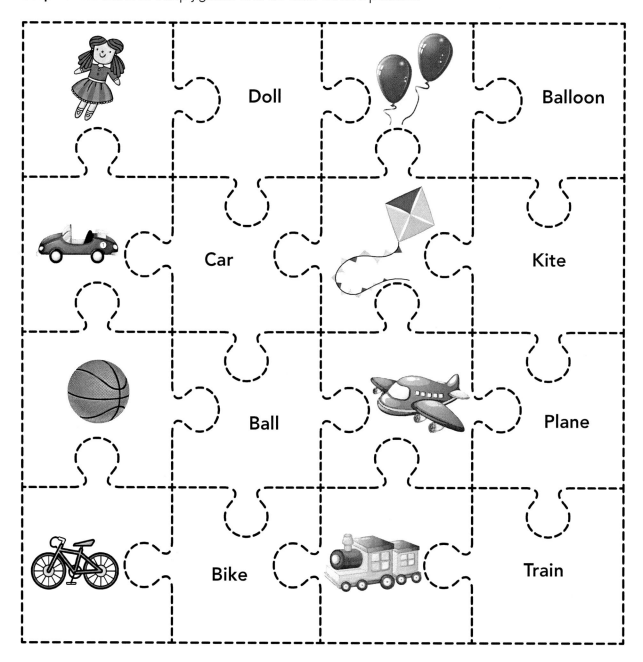

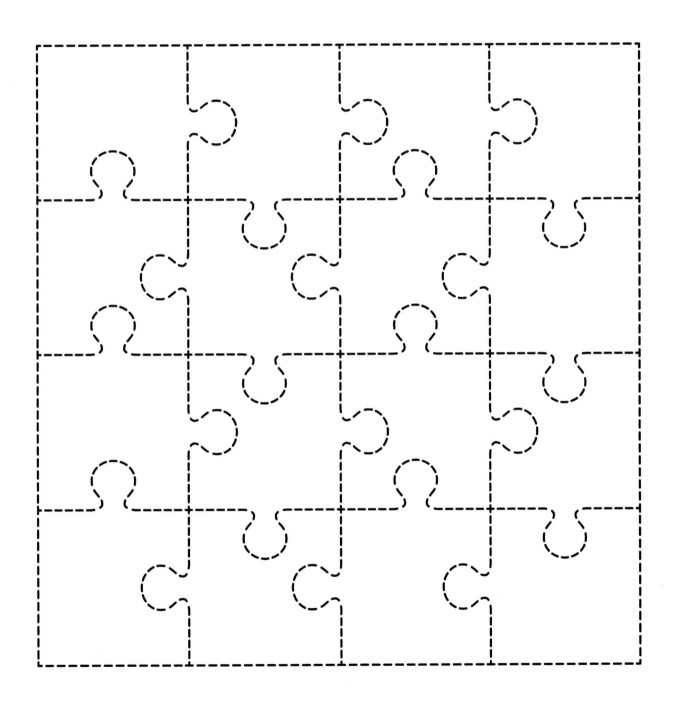

Name: _____   Class: _____   Date: _____

Find 10 differences

Bedroom 1

In bedroom 1 there _____

_____

_____

_____

_____

_____

Unit 39, point 5: 'Spot the difference' worksheet 2

Name: _____ Class: _____ Date: _____

Bedroom 2

In bedroom 2 there _____

_____

_____

_____

_____

_____

Unit 39, point 6: Counting worksheet

Name: _____ Class: _____ Date: _____

My toys

Look and write.
How many toys are there?

□	□	□	□	□	□

_____ _____ _____ _____ _____ _____

 Appendix

Name: _____   Class: _____   Date: _____

Colour by numbers

Look and colour.

yellow

red

blue

purple

green

orange

Japanese doll

Scottish doll

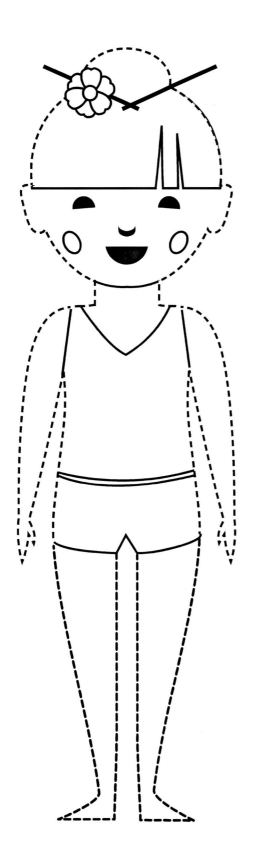

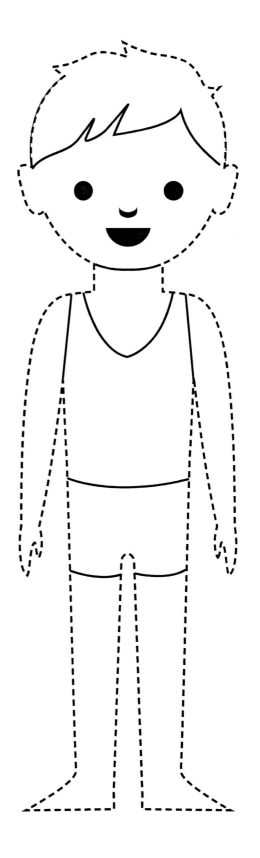

 Appendix

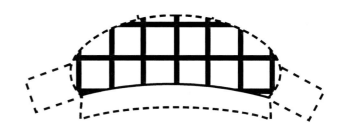

Unit 40, point 5: 'Listen and draw' monster worksheet

A full colour version of this material is available at https://www.myetpedia.com/appendix-materials/

Name: _____ Class: _____ Date: _____

Monster A

1. Describe your monster to your partner.

2. Listen and draw your partner's monster.

ETpedia: Young Learners © Pavilion Publishing and Media Ltd and its licensors 2016. **Appendix**

Name: _____ Class: _____ Date: _____

Monster B

1. Describe your monster to your partner.

2. Listen and draw your partner's monster.

A full colour version of this material is available at https://www.myetpedia.com/appendix-materials/

Create a monster

ETpedia: Young Learners © Pavilion Publishing and Media Ltd and its licensors 2016.

Appendix

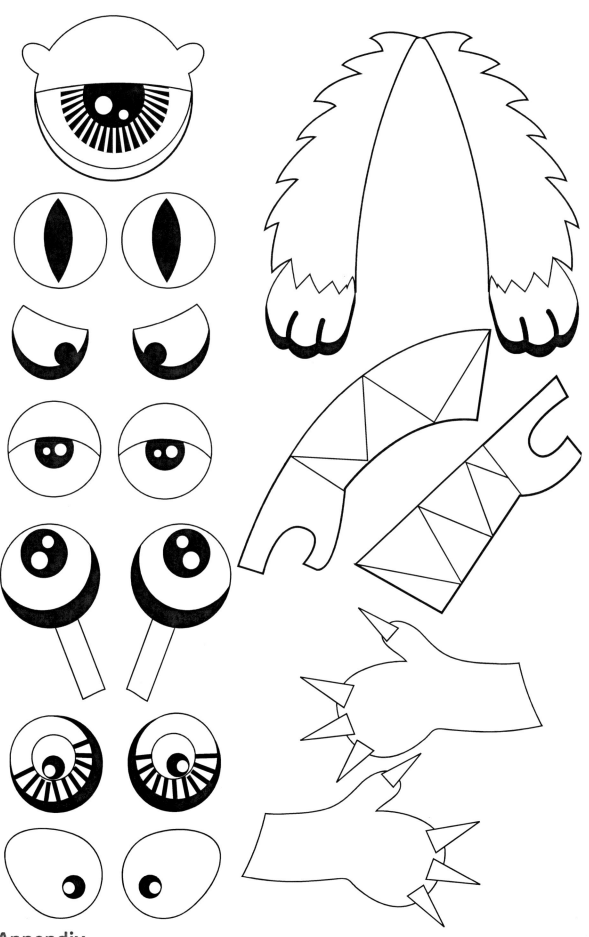

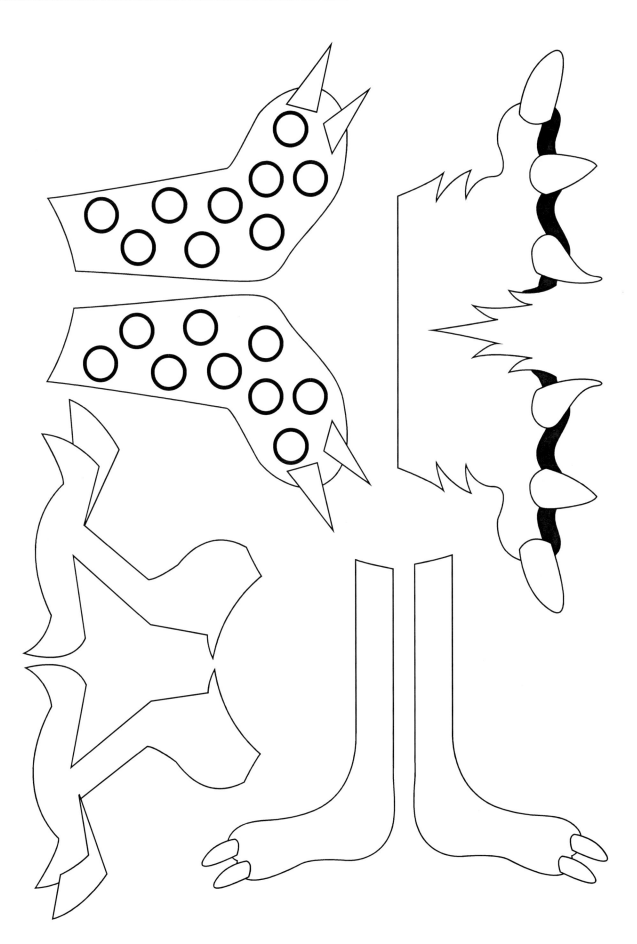

Unit 40, point 8: 'Who's who?' game

Name: _____ Class: _____ Date: _____

Who's who?

| Nick | Bill | Ann | Lucy | Grace |

| John | Sam | Sue | Kim | Ben |

| Dan | Pat | Alex | Anna | Tony |

 Appendix

Nick

He's middle aged.
He has got short
brown hair and
brown eyes.
He wears glasses.
His face is round.
He's chubby.
His eyes are small.

Bill

He's old.
He is a bit bald.
He has got a
white beard.
He's thin.
He's got an oval face.
His eyes are small and blue.

Ann

He's young.
She's pretty.
She's got short,
curly blonde hair.
She's thin.
She has got an oval face.
She has got big brown eyes.

Lucy

She's young.
She's pretty.
She's got long,
straight black hair.
Her face is long.
She's got big brown eyes.

Grace

She's old.
She's got short,
wavy light
brown hair.
She wears glasses.
Her face is round.
She's got small brown eyes.

John

He's old.
He's bald.
He wears glasses.
He's got small
black eyes.
He's a bit fat.

Sam

He's young and
handsome.
He's got short,
curly black hair.
He has got big black eyes.
His face is oval.
He's elegant.

Sue

She's middle aged.
She's pretty.
She has got
glasses.
She's got shoulder length
straight red hair.
She has got big green eyes
and a long face.

Kim

She's old.
She's got short
wavy blonde hair.
She's got big blue
eyes and big eyelashes.
She's ugly.
Her face is oval.

Ben

He's young.
He's thin.
He's got short,
curly blond hair.
He's got small
blue eyes.
His face is round.

Dan

He's young.
He's got a
round face.
He's got freckles.
He wears glasses.
He's got short wavy brown hair
and small brown eyes.

Pat

She's young and
pretty.
She's got long
brown curly hair.
She's got pigtails.
Her face is long.
She has got big black eyes.

Alex

He's a teenager.
He's got a
round face.
He's got
brown eyes.
He's got very short hair.
His hair is brown.
It is straight.

Anna

She's young
and pretty.
She's got wavy
black hair.
Her eyes are black.
She has got a long face.
She is slim.

Tony

He's wearing
a red cap.
He's got long
brown hair.
It is in a ponytail.
His face is oval.
He's got small brown eyes.

Name: _____ Class: _____ Date: _____

The secret body code

1. Look and write. Then draw.

✂	📖	☎	✉	🖱	📄	⊙	👌	☺	✡	☯	♉	&
a	b	c	d	e	f	g	h	i	j	k	l	m

◆	⌘	➑	⊙	★	➯	✿	⌫	🎧	②	☑	◀	🕐
n	o	p	q	r	s	t	u	v	w	x	y	z

1	2	3
👌🖱✂✉ _ _ _ _	🖱◀🖱➯ _ _ _ _	&⌘⌫✿👌 _ _ _ _ _
4 ✂★&➯ _ _ _ _	**5** 🖱✂★➯ _ _ _ _	**6** 👌✂◆✉➯ _ _ _ _ _
7 ♉🖱⊙➯ _ _ _ _	**8** ➯👌⌘⌫♉✉🖱★➯ _ _ _ _ _ _ _ _ _	**9** ✿⌫&&◀ _ _ _ _ _

 Appendix

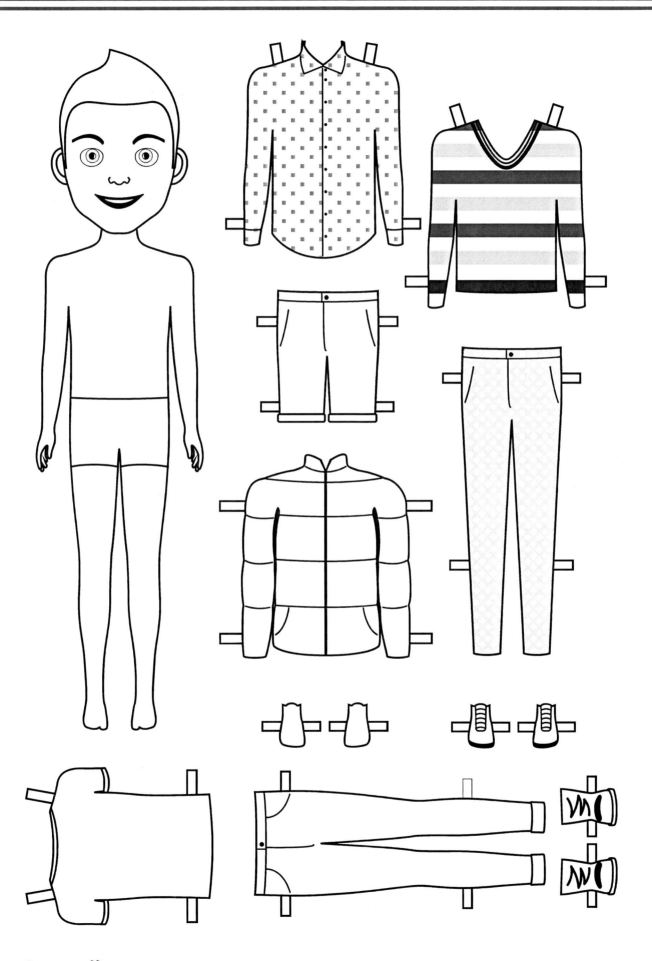

Appendix

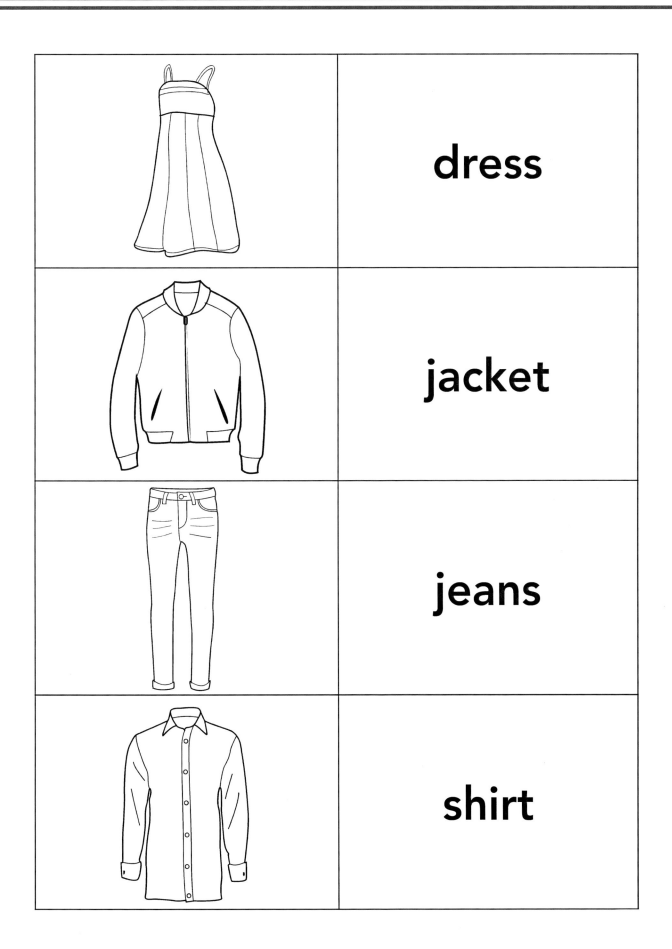

	dress
	jacket
	jeans
	shirt

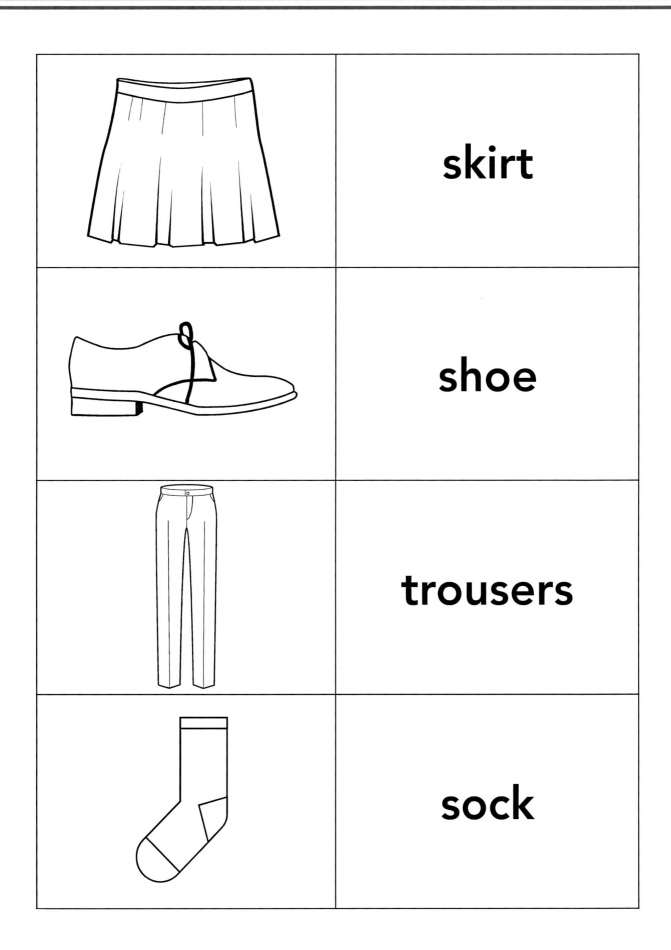

	skirt
	shoe
	trousers
	sock

   Appendix

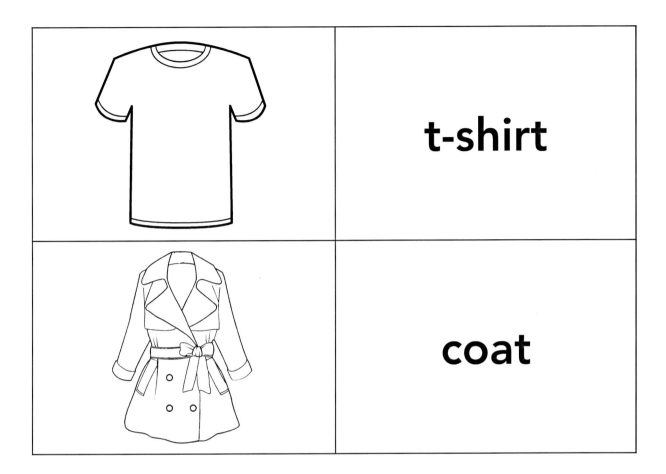

| | t-shirt |
| coat |

Unit 41, point 3: Clothes word search

Name: _____ Class: _____ Date: _____

Topic: _____

1. Find these words:

DRESS   JEANS   TROUSERS   SWEATER   HAT

SHIRT   COAT   SKIRT   SCARF

A	D	R	E	S	S	I	C	H	S
J	U	T	F	L	K	R	L	K	W
Y	X	C	J	P	I	O	M	S	E
E	L	N	X	R	R	T	D	C	A
R	D	C	O	A	T	B	H	A	T
J	E	A	N	S	I	W	K	R	E
L	K	N	Z	H	F	F	Y	F	R
R	P	S	H	I	R	T	L	B	P
J	L	W	B	N	M	K	L	O	P
T	R	O	U	S	E	R	S	R	M

 Appendix

2. Now write the words and draw a picture of each.

1.	2.
3.	4.
5.	6.
7.	8.
9.	10.

Answer key:

A	D	R	E	S	S	I	C	H	S
J	U	T	F	L	K	R	L	K	W
Y	X	C	J	P	I	O	M	S	E
E	L	N	X	R	R	T	D	C	A
R	D	C	O	A	T	B	H	A	T
J	E	A	N	S	I	W	K	R	E
L	K	N	Z	H	F	F	Y	F	R
R	P	S	H	I	R	T	L	B	P
J	L	W	B	N	M	K	L	O	P
T	R	O	U	S	E	R	S	R	M

Unit 41, point 3 contd.: Blank template for word search

Name: _____ Class: _____ Date: _____

Topic: _____

1. Find these words:

_____ _____ _____ _____ _____

_____ _____ _____ _____ _____

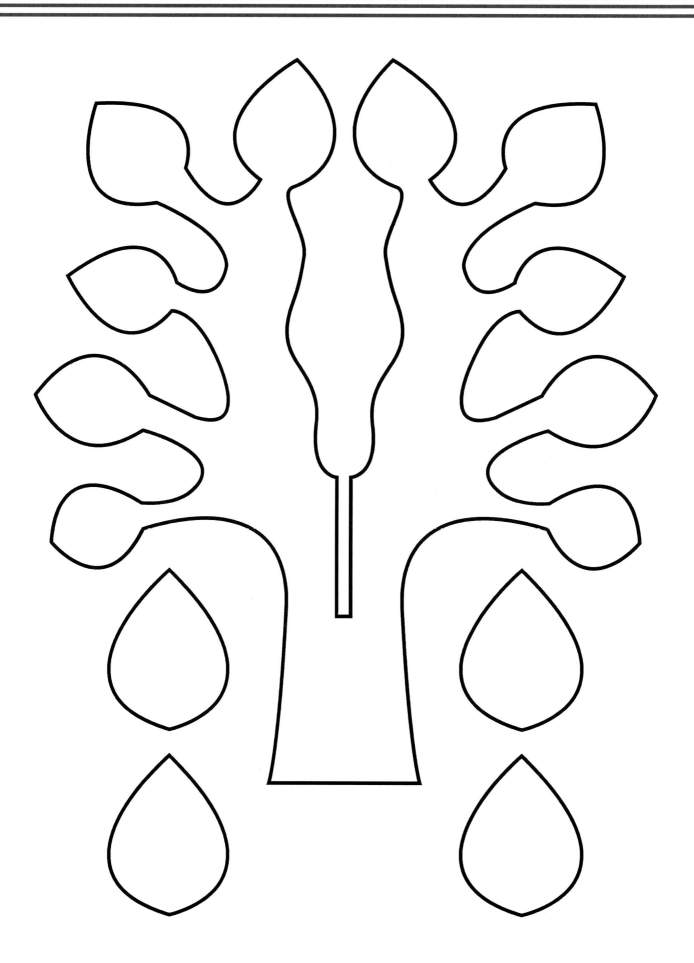

 Appendix

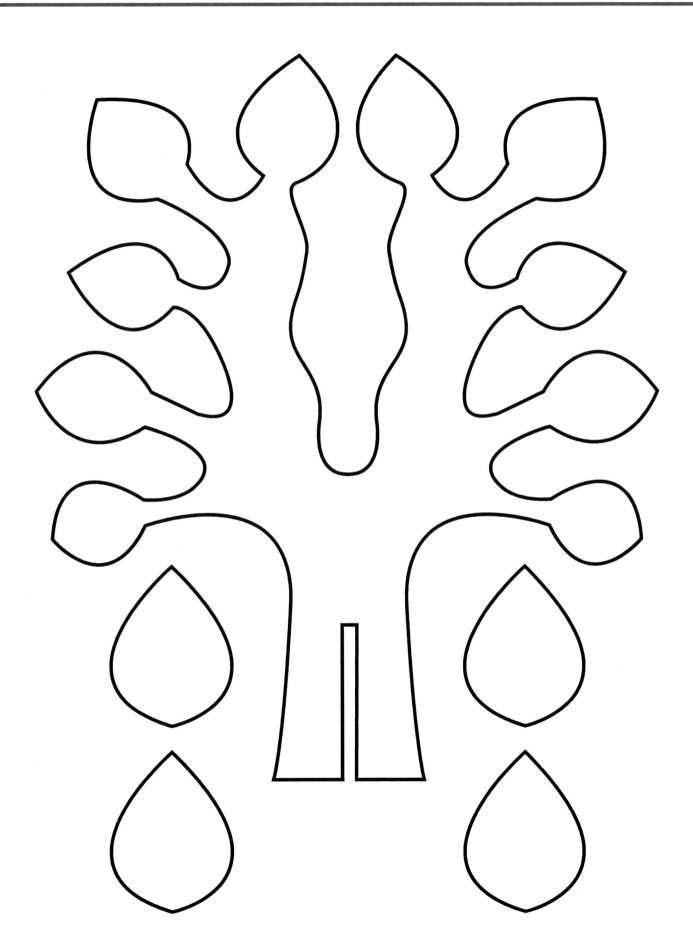

A full colour version of this material is available at https://www.myetpedia.com/appendix-materials/

ETpedia: Young Learners © Pavilion Publishing and Media Ltd and its licensors 2016.   **Appendix**

Unit 42, point 2: Listening activity

A full colour version of this material is available at https://www.myetpedia.com/appendix-materials/

Name : _____   Date: _____

My family

1. Listen and draw lines from the people to their place on the tree.

This is my family. My grandmother's name is Pat and she has got white hair and glasses. That's right. My grandmother has got white hair and glasses.

And my grandfather's name is Ben. He has got grey hair and glasses. That's right. My grandfather Ben has got grey hair and glasses.

My mother's name is Grace and she is slim. She has got black hair. Yes, my mother is tall and slim and she has got black hair.

Look at my father. His name is Tom. He has got blond hair and glasses. That's right. My father, Tom, has got blond hair and glasses.

Look at my brother. His name is Nick. He is wearing trousers and a t-shirt. Yes, that's right. My brother Nick is wearing trousers and a t-shirt.

And that's my sister. Her name is May. She has got pigtails. Yes, my sister May has got pigtails.

And that's me. My name's Alex and I'm wearing shorts and trainers. Yes, my name is Alex and I'm wearing shorts and trainers. I love my family!

Unit 42, point 8: Family counting worksheet

Name: _____ Class: _____ Date: _____

How many people are there?

1.

    ┌─┐
    └┐├
     ┴

    Four

There are four people in this family.

There are four people in this family.

2.

    ┌──────┐
    │ ── │
    │ ──── │
    │ ── │
    └──────┘

    _____
    _____
    _____

There are _____ people in this family.

_____
_____

3.

    ┌──────┐
    │ ── │
    │ ──── │
    │ ── │
    └──────┘

    _____
    _____
    _____

There are _____ people in this family.

_____
_____

4. My family

There are _____ people in my family.

Unit 43, point 5: Decorate a room

A full colour version of this material is available at https://www.myetpedia.com/appendix-materials/

Name: _____ Class: _____ Date: _____

1. Cut out the furniture and write the words. Then decorate the living room.

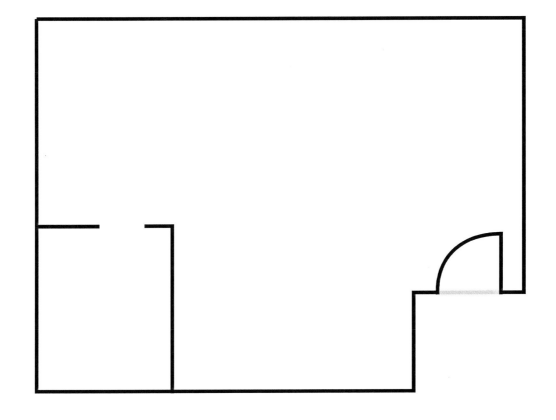

Listening text:

In the living room there is a sofa. Can you see the sofa? Good! Colour the sofa blue. It's a blue sofa.

Now, can you see the cushions? Good! Put the cushions on the sofa. Yes, put the yellow cushions on the sofa. That's right. The cushions are yellow.

Look at the TV. Can you see the TV? The TV is black. Put the TV on the table.

Now can you see the orange lamp? Put the orange lamp on the table next to the TV.

✄ -

Name: _____   Class: _____   Date: _____

Listen, draw lines and colour in.

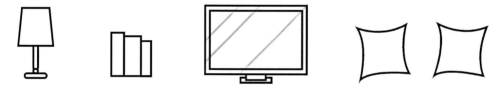

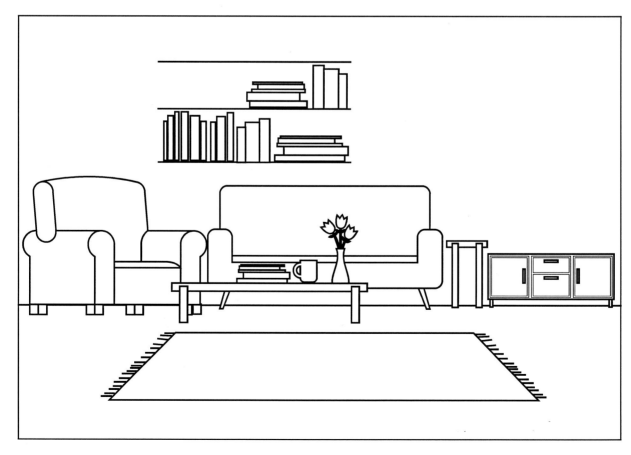

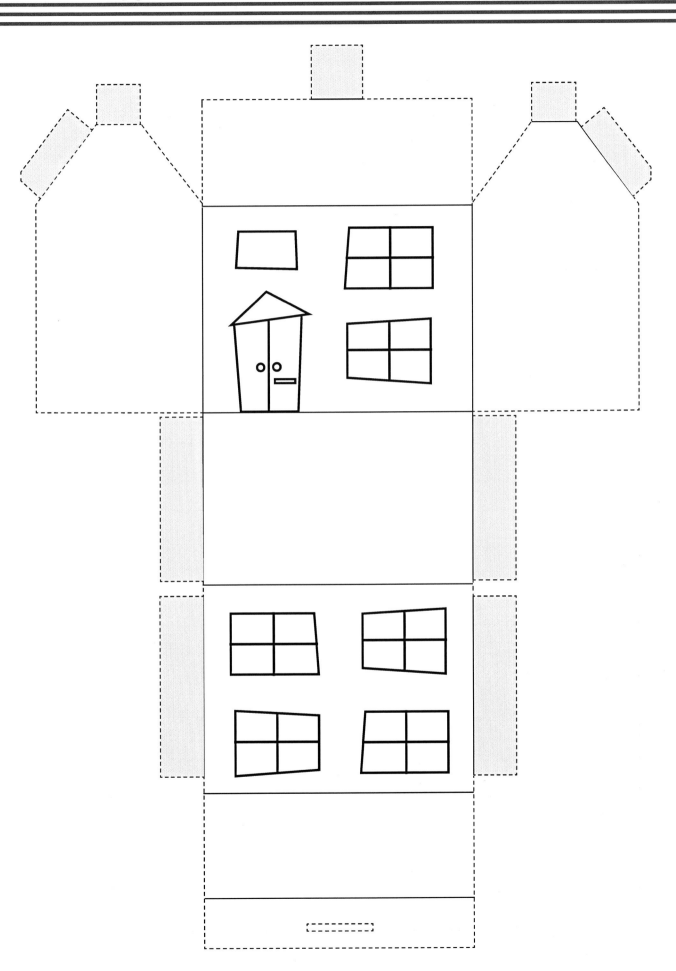

Unit 43, point 8: House battleships

A full colour version of this material is available at https://www.myetpedia.com/appendix-materials/

Name: _____ Class: _____ Date: _____

House battleships

1. Ask and answer the questions below and play battleships.

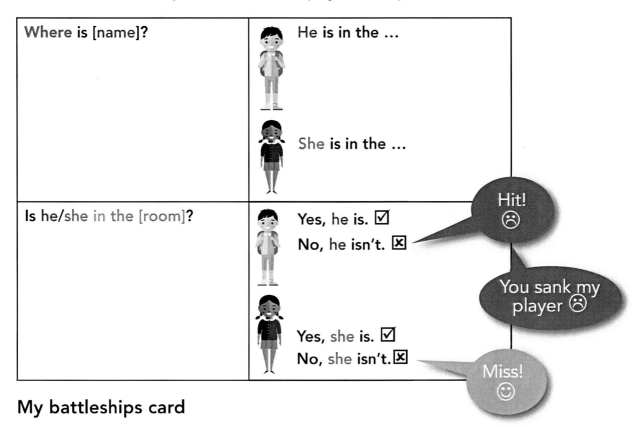

My battleships card

		A	B	C	D	E	F	G	H	I
		living room	dining room	hall	kitchen	toilet	bedroom	bathroom	attic	garage
1	Alex									
2	Grace									
3	Dan									
4	Pat									
5	Nick									
6	Tony									

Appendix

My house

I live in a house. It is a big house. It has got a beautiful garden. There are two trees in the garden and lots of pretty flowers.

There are two floors in my house.

On the ground floor there is a big living room, a big dining room, a kitchen, a study and a small hall near the front door.

On the first floor there are three bedrooms and two bathrooms. My parents' room has got a bathroom but I share a bathroom with my brother.

My house is very cosy. I love my house.

Name: _____ Class: _____ Date: _____

1. Join the dots. Then write and colour in.

Name: _____ Class: _____ Date: _____

1. Join the dots. Then write and colour in.

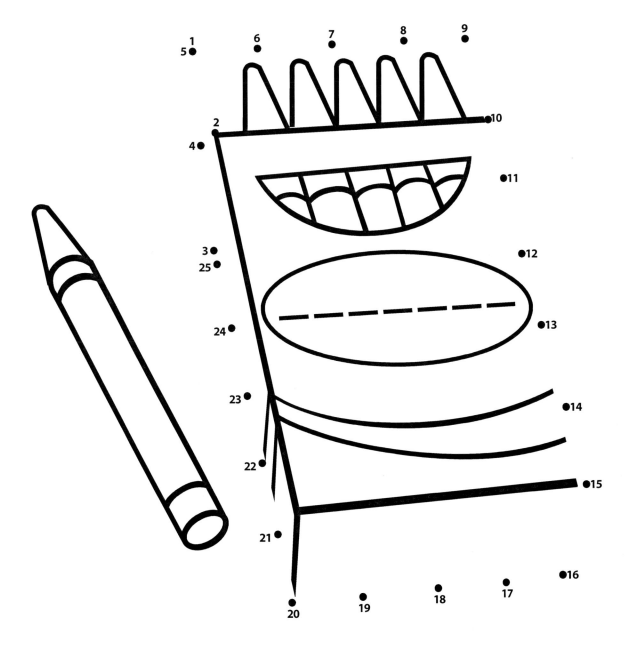

Unit 44, point 2: Link and trace

Name: _____ Class: _____ Date: _____

1. Join the pictures and the words. Then trace and colour in.

paper

backpack

writing

board

chair

student

book

desk

teacher

globe

Appendix

Unit 46, point 2: The perfect pancake

Name: _____ Class: _____ Date: _____

Shrove Tuesday (Pancake Day)

1. Draw your favourite pancake toppings. Then colour.

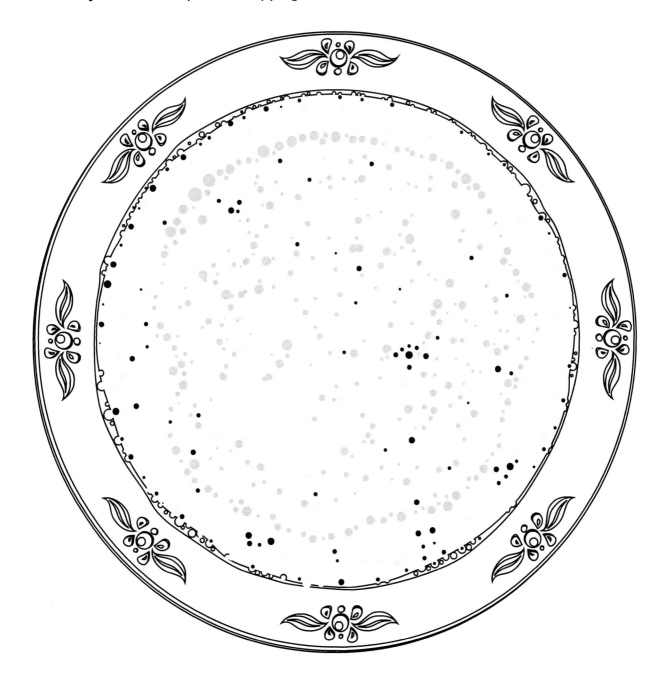

Observation form for Unit _____

Name	Asks relevant questions	Makes relevant comments	Follows directions	Works autonomously	Knows the meaning of target vocabulary	Recognises target vocabulary	Applies target vocabulary correctly	Spells target vocabulary correctly

 Appendix

Unit 48, point 1: Progress chart

Classroom Progress chart

Unit : _____

Topic: _____

Target vocabulary for the unit: _____

Name	Reading		Writing		Listening		Speaking		
	Read + understand a short text	Answer comprehension questions on the text	Write sentences with the target vocabulary	Write a short text about: ___	Listen to and understand a short text	Answer comprehension questions on the listening	Understand instructions	Pronounce the target vocabulary correctly	Answer questions on the topic	Interact with others on the topic

Class observation/behaviour chart

Draw a ☑ for positive behaviour or a ☒ according to the behaviour observed in each category for each student.

Name	Talkative	Co-operative with : T	Co-operative with : SS	Follows classroom rules	Concentrates	Participates in class	Appropriate social behaviour	Punctual	Brings classroom materials	Does homework

Appendix

Name: _____   Class: _____

Level: _____   Term: _____

Term Report

Behaviour

	☑	☒
is co-operative		
follows classroom rules		
concentrates		
participates in class		
has appropriate social behaviour		
is punctual		
brings materials required		
does set homework		

Recommendation:

Next term, _____ should work on improving:

_____

and continue to: _____

Marks:

Test 1	
Test 2	
Show and tell	
Project work/Groupwork	
Final mark	

Recommendation:

Next term, _____ should work on improving:

_____

and continue to: _____

Unit 48, point 6: Term report

1. _____

2. _____

3. _____

Overall teacher's comment	Overall parent's comment

Date: _____ / _____ / _____

Teacher: _____

         Appendix

Unit 48, point 7: Skills report

Name: _____ Class: _____

Level: _____ Term: _____

Responsibility		Organisation	
1. Is always responsible	☐	1. Is always organised	☐
2. Is usually responsible	☐	2. Is usually organised	☐
3. Is rarely responsible	☐	3. Is rarely organised	☐
Independent work		**Collaboration**	
1. Usually works independently	☐	1. Always collaborates with others	☐
2. Usually requires teacher's/a peer's help	☐	2. Usually collaborates with others	☐
		3. Is not yet able to collaborate with others	☐
General strengths			
1. Does neat and thorough work			☐
2. Usually tries to do his/her best			☐
3. Takes instructions well and instantly applies them			☐
4. Is motivated and hardworking			☐
5. _____			☐

Main unit objectives for the skill

	Outstanding	Satisfactory	Needs improving
1. Listening: recognises and understands target vocabulary.			
2. Speaking: uses target vocabulary correctly.			
3. Reading: recognises and understands target vocabulary in short written texts.			
4. Writing: spells and writes sentences/short texts with target vocabulary correctly			
5._____			

Specific skill strengths demonstrated	Areas to work on
1	1
2	2

Unit 48, point 7: Skills report

Name: _____   Class: _____

Level: _____   Term: _____

Student feedback

My best work is:	My goal for improvement is:
Student's signature	_____

Parent feedback

I have read and received this report.	I'd like to discuss this report. **Contact details:** Landline: _____ Mobile: _____ Contact hours: _____
Parent's signature	_____

Write your own 10 tips

ETpedia: Young Learners © Pavilion Publishing and Media Ltd and its licensors 2016.

Write your own 10 tips

Appendix

Write your own 10 tips

Write your own 10 tips

 Appendix

Write your own 10 tips